HOCKEY'S TOP 100

DON WEEKES

and

KERRY BANKS

HOCKEY'S TOP 100

The

GAME'S GREATEST RECORDS

GREYSTONE BOOKS

Douglas & McIntyre Publishing Group

Vancouver/Toronto/Berkeley

For Caroline, Katie and Alex—Don Weekes
For my daughter, Riley—Kerry Banks

Copyright © 2008 by Don Weekes and Kerry Banks

08 09 10 11 12   5 4 3 2

Greystone Books
A division of Douglas & McIntyre Ltd.
2323 Quebec Street, Suite 201
Vancouver, British Columbia
Canada V5T 4S7
www.greystonebooks.com

Library and Archives Canada Cataloguing in Publication
Weekes, Don
Hockey's top 100 : the game's greatest records / Don Weekes, Kerry Banks.

ISBN 978-1-55365-274-8

1. National Hockey League—Miscellanea. 2. Hockey—Records.
3. Hockey—Miscellanea. I. Banks, Kerry, 1952– II. Title.
III. Title: Hockey's top one hundred.
GV847.8.N3W425 2008   796.962'64   C2008-900379-9

Editing by Anne Rose
Cover design by Peter Cocking and Jessica Sullivan
Text design by Jessica Sullivan
Cover photos by Hockey Hall of Fame
Printed and bound in China by C & C Offset Printing Co., Ltd.
Printed on acid-free paper
Distributed in the U.S. by Publishers Group West

We gratefully acknowledge the financial support of the Canada Council for the Arts,
the British Columbia Arts Council, the Province of British Columbia through
the Book Publishing Tax Credit, and the Government of Canada through the
Book Publishing Industry Development Program (BPIDP) for our publishing activities.

INTRODUCTION

Let's establish one thing up front. We knew that selecting the top 100 NHL records wasn't going to be easy. After all, there is no proven scientific method of evaluating the individual merits of offensive and defensive achievements. This holds true for hockey, baseball, football—and any other sport. So why step out on thin ice? Frankly, the sheer challenge of the idea appealed to us.

To arrive at our rankings we employed several objective standards, such as a record's longevity, its chances of remaining unbroken, its historical impact and its margin of domination. Yet, even with these benchmarks, we had trouble reaching a consensus. We butted heads over many choices. We even had conflicting opinions on a few records that were eventually cut from the list. By necessity then, the final order represents a compromise between our positions.

We differed sharply, for example, on how high to rank single-game standards, such as Bill Mosienko's sizzling 21-second hat trick and Darryl Sittler's miraculous 10-point night. How can you equate what a player accomplishes in one game with what another achieves over the course of a season or career? In the cases of Mosienko and Sittler there was a fluke factor involved—both records were achieved against goalies who were rookie second-stringers. Even so, no one has duplicated either of these amazing feats. And more than a few subpar netminders have been run through the NHL wringer by snipers wielding a hot Victoriaville.

We also found it difficult to gauge the importance of records established in different eras. Do the 22 shutouts that goaltender George Hainsworth posted in 1928–29 (during an era when forward passing was prohibited and nine of the 10 NHL teams averaged less than two goals per game) represent a greater achievement than the modern-day mark of 15 zeroes racked up by rookie Tony Esposito in 1969–70? If so, it is certainly not by much.

Another problem was posed by Wayne Gretzky. The Great One still owns 60 official individual NHL records (of his original 61 since retirement) and a few dozen more that are not recognized. One of those unofficial marks—fewest games needed to score 50 goals from the start of a season—appears in our top 10. We could easily have highlighted more than seven of Gretzky's multitude of records, but, at the risk of making this book a tribute to No. 99, we had to draw the line somewhere.

Several other unofficial records earned a place in our personal top 100, including the 1972–73 New York Rangers' unknown feat of scoring 25 unanswered goals and goalie Kirk McLean's overlooked gem of 761 saves in one playoff year. Another unofficial record—most goals without a power-play goal in one season—gave us a chance to shine the spotlight on one of the NHL's most obscure performers: Moose Jaw's Doug Smail. Although some hockey purists may object, we also included a few notable penalty records. They may not symbolize talent, but they do stand as a testament to intestinal fortitude and focussed fury. As well, we reserved a spot on the roster for a few remarkable coaching exploits and some age-related milestones set by the likes of Gordie Howe, Bill Cook and Sidney Crosby.

So, what makes a record truly great? You are about to find out.

Don Weekes and Kerry Banks
January 2008

1

MOST POINTS IN A CAREER

2,857: *Wayne Gretzky, 1979–80 to 1998–99*

This is hockey's biggest number, hands down. How big is it exactly? Well, consider that Mark Messier, the NHL's second-highest scorer with 1,887 career points, posted 970 fewer points than Wayne Gretzky, while Hall of Famers Bobby Orr, Maurice Richard and Ted Lindsay didn't even amass 970 points in the course of their careers. If we were to count only Gretzky's assists (1,973), he would still lead Messier by 86 points. And Gretzky's total doesn't include the 382 points that he piled up in 208 playoff games. Add those to the mix and we are up to a colossal 3,239 points. Need more evidence? Try to wrap your mind around the fact that Gretzky became the NHL's all-time leading scorer when he was just 28 years old, and the fact that he averaged 1.92 points per game over his 20-year NHL career, a number that takes on even more weight when you consider that only four other players in NHL history have posted higher points-per-game averages in a single season. Career milestones may often lack the dazzle of individual game or single-season exploits, but we have to genuflect before this baby. It speaks volumes about Gretzky's excellence, drive and longevity. This record won't be broken. This record stands alone.

MOST CONSECUTIVE TOP-FIVE FINISHES
IN THE REGULAR-SEASON SCORING RACE

20: Gordie Howe, Detroit Red Wings, 1949–50 to 1968–69

While Gordie Howe's 26-season NHL record may be beatable (as Mark Messier nearly proved), there is slim chance of anyone ever challenging Mr. Hockey's top-five finishes in the scoring race. Longevity, combined with offensive excellence and consistency, is a hallmark of Howe's astonishing five-decade career. Remarkably, in 20 of 26 NHL seasons, he finished fifth or better in league scoring. And he did it the hard way—consecutively. Howe began his string in 1949–50, with 68 points and a third-place showing behind linemates Ted Lindsay and Sid Abel. He then won the next four Art Ross Trophies, followed by another two scoring titles. His run was almost broken in 1959–60, when he finished just eight points back of leader Bobby Hull and tied Henri Richard for fifth overall. During the stretch, he ranked second once, had five third-place showings, two fourth-place finishes and six placings in fifth. Still, though a few players topped him in points, no one ever beat him with any real consistency. As with Wayne Gretzky, his greatest competition was usually himself. Howe was almost invincible through three generations of superstars, from Maurice Richard to Bobby Hull to Phil Esposito, while scoring 1,583 points—an average of almost 80 points per season for 20 years.

MOST CONSECUTIVE COMPLETE GAMES
PLAYED BY A GOALIE (INCLUDING PLAYOFFS)

551: Glenn Hall, 1955–56 to 1962–63

A seven-time First Team All-Star, Glenn Hall is famous for pioneering the butterfly style of goaltending as well as for his pre-game vomiting ritual. But Hall didn't view regurgitation as a handicap. As the Hall of Famer put it, "When I threw up, I felt I was doing what I needed to do to prepare for the game. I felt that if I threw up, I played better." The gut-wrenching rite didn't keep the courageous Chicago goaltender out of the lineup, either. In fact, Hall's mental toughness, luck and lightning-fast reflexes enabled him to survive more than six seasons of flying pucks and flashing sticks without incurring a serious injury. Between the start of the 1955–56 season until back spasms finally forced him to leave in the first period of a contest against Boston on November 7, 1962, Hall played 502 consecutive, complete regular-season games plus 49 playoff games—a span of more than 33,000 minutes without a break. Even more incredible, Hall accomplished this ironman feat while playing without a mask and using rudimentary equipment that would not pass safety regulations today. When people talk about hockey's most unbreakable records, this monster tops the list.

39: Wayne Gretzky, Edmonton Oilers, 1981–82

Among Wayne Gretzky's array of scoring milestones, he considers this one his most precious. As he once told the *Edmonton Journal*, it's "my favourite because I think it will be the hardest to break." Prior to Gretzky, only Maurice Richard and Mike Bossy had scored 50 goals in 50 games, and both did it in the last few minutes of their 50th game. But in 1981–82, with Edmonton ruthlessly mauling its opponents, the 20-year-old set his sights on the mark. Passing less and shooting more, he fired a career-high 369 shots on net. Gretzky scored his 40th goal in Game 36 versus Calgary, got number 41 in the next game against Vancouver, then scored four times in a 10–3 blitz of Los Angeles for 45 goals in 38 games. Then on December 30, versus Philadelphia, he hit the mark in spectacular style, putting four pucks past Pete Peeters before sliding his fifth of the night, and his 50th of the season, into an empty net to seal a 7–5 win. After the game, in defiance of NHL protocol, Flyers captain Bobby Clarke went into Edmonton's dressing room to tell Gretzky, "I know everything that's been written about you. I think none of it is adequate." Gretzky had scored 50 goals before the season's midway mark. Riding that momentum, he went on to post an NHL-record 92 goals.

MOST SHUTOUTS IN A CAREER

103: Terry Sawchuk, 1949–50 to 1969–70

92: Martin Brodeur, 1991–92 to 2006–07

Terry Sawchuk's stratospheric 103 shutouts was once considered one of hockey's most impregnable records. Only old-timer George Hainsworth, at 94, was remotely close to Sawchuk's milestone, which was built on the back of an astounding 65 shutouts in his first six seasons. Then, Lou Lamoriello drafted Martin Brodeur 20th overall for New Jersey in 1990. The Montreal-born puck stopper joined a team that emphasized defensive play and he soon began chipping away at Sawchuk's hallowed mark. By the end of 2003–04, the 32-year-old had compiled 75 whitewashes, and Sawchuk's record suddenly seemed vulnerable. Brodeur has been aided in pursuit of Sawchuk by playing in an era in which NHL scoring nosedived, but his shutout total is also a product of his incredible durability. In 11 seasons from 1995–96 to 2006–07, he appeared in 89 per cent (800 of 902) of the Devils' games. Entering 2007–08, Brodeur had logged 92 shutouts and, barring a career-ending injury, he looks certain not only to surpass Sawchuk but to push the record out of reach of any future goaltender. "It is without a doubt going to be his most incredible record," noted former NHL goalie Glenn "Chico" Resch. "It's going to be like Wayne Gretzky's 92 goals in a season."

6

HIGHEST PLUS-MINUS IN ONE SEASON

124: Bobby Orr, Boston Bruins, 1970–71

This is one of those rare records that has "unbreakable" stamped all over it. The plus-minus rating is a statistical attempt to combine a player's offensive and defensive contributions to his team at even strength. The higher the rating, the better, and no one ever pushed it higher than Bobby Orr, who led the NHL in the category a record six times before knee miseries forced his retirement. But Boston's wonderboy really engaged the afterburners in 1970–71, when he posted a colossal plus-124. In today's game, a player who attains a score of 50 is thought to be excelling. In comparison, Wayne Gretzky's best rating was a plus-98, in 1984–85, when he scored 208 points. Larry Robinson is the only other player to top the 100 plateau—a plus-120, with Montreal in 1976–77. Not only does Orr own the highest plus-minus ever recorded in one season, his career plus-minus average works out to an amazing .91 (nearly a goal per game), a number that leaves everyone else in the dust. Orr's average is almost twice as high as the second-best player, Robinson, at .53; no one else even tops .45. As former Boston general manager Milt Schmidt said about Orr, "Every time he was on that ice, the opposition would be playing a man short."

7

MOST CONSECUTIVE STANLEY CUPS WON BY A TEAM

5: Montreal Canadiens, 1956 to 1960

The dynasty that the Club de Hockey Canadien built in the mid-1950s was a product of savvy management, a strong farm system, top-calibre coaching and a virtual monopoly on French-Canadian talent. And though there is no doubt it was easier to dominate when the NHL was composed of only six teams rather than 30, Montreal did have to overcome some stiff competition from the Detroit Red Wings. After winning the Cup in 1953, Montreal was defeated by Detroit in hard-fought seven-game finals in 1954 and 1955. If not for those two Game 7 losses, Montreal might have assembled a string of eight straight Cups. But after finally putting Detroit away in the 1956 finals, the Habs began to take command, a trend that coincided with the emergence of Jean Béliveau as the league's elite centre. The lineup was deep and solid. In all, 12 players—known as "the Apostles"—would skate for all five Cup-winning squads. And during its record-setting five-year reign, Montreal never trailed in a playoff series and was never pushed to a Game 7 while averaging more then 40 wins per campaign and winning four league titles. The fantastic run finally ended in Game 6 of the 1961 semifinals amid the smoky din of Chicago Stadium, when the first-place Canadiens were upset by the third-place Chicago Blackhawks.

MOST POINTS IN ONE SEASON

215: Wayne Gretzky, Edmonton Oilers, 1985–86

In discussing his most impressive scoring feats, Wayne Gretzky once observed, "I think 163 assists in a season will be hard to beat; that and 215 points." Indeed, such supernatural numbers appear to be beyond the reach of mere mortals. As of 2007, only two other NHLers besides Gretzky have topped 100 assists in a season (Mario Lemieux, with 114 in 1988–89, and Bobby Orr, with 102 in 1970–71), while no other player has ever managed to collect 200 points in a season. The 215 points that Gretzky put on the board for Edmonton in 1985–86 was a mind-boggling 74 points more than second-place Lemieux tallied. Even if he had not netted a single goal all year, Gretzky's assists alone would have given him the scoring crown. Making players around him better was a Gretzky hallmark. It's no accident that he owns the NHL's top seven single-season assist totals. His 215-point output in 1985–86 was the Great One's third consecutive 200-point campaign, and for all intents and purposes he had run out of single-season scoring records to track down. At age 25, the spindly centre was the unquestioned king of the hill. "He's made the record book obsolete," marvelled Minnesota general manager Lou Nanne. "His only point of reference is himself."

MOST GOALS BY A DEFENSEMAN IN ONE SEASON

48: Paul Coffey, Edmonton Oilers, 1985–86

When Bobby Orr ripped home 46 goals in 1974–75 to set a new single-season record for defensemen, it didn't seem possible that anyone would challenge the mark. After all, to that point no other blueliner had scored even 30 goals in a season. But the impossible became reality 11 years later, when Paul Coffey stunned the hockey world by scoring 48. It's true that Coffey benefited from playing during the goal-crazy 1980s, but there is no disputing his puckhandling talents and sportscar speed. "He moves like a marble on a hardwood floor," quipped *Toronto Sun* sportswriter Jim O'Leary. Perhaps the finest skater of his era, Coffey quarterbacked the Oilers' power play and functioned as a fourth forward in the team's potent run-and-gun attack. In 1983–84, he scored 40 goals and collected 126 points, second only to Wayne Gretzky in the NHL scoring race. Two years later, Coffey took his game to a higher level and eclipsed Orr's record, netting his 47th goal on a rink-length dash against Vancouver in the third-last game of the season. He finished the year with 138 points on 48 goals and 90 assists. Remarkably, Coffey broke Orr's hallowed mark despite counting only nine power-play goals, seven less than the 16 Orr scored in 1974–75.

MOST POINTS IN ONE GAME

10: Darryl Sittler, Toronto Maple Leafs, February 7, 1976

It is still hard to fathom how Darryl Sittler did it. Toronto's opponents, the Boston Bruins, were no pushovers—they had lost only once in their last 17 games. The Leafs' lone edge was in net: Gilles Gilbert, Boston's top goalie, was injured, and though the club had just reacquired Gerry Cheevers from the WHA, coach Don Cherry opted to start rookie Dave Reece. After getting two assists in the first period, Sittler caught fire in the second, scoring three goals and two assists to give him seven points. Between periods, the Toronto captain had been told he was one point shy of the NHL mark for most points in a game, held by Maurice Richard and Bert Olmstead. He had 20 minutes to get one point to tie the record or two points to break it. Incredibly, he got three—all goals. The record-setter came midway through the period. Corralling the puck just inside Boston's blue line, Sittler spun away from a pair of checkers and wired a snap shot past Reece. A few shifts later, while standing behind the Boston net, Sittler made a pass to a teammate. The puck deflected off the skates of two Bruin defenders and bounced through Reece's legs. He had scored his sixth goal and 10th point. The Leafs won the game 11–4. "It was a night when every time I had the puck, something seemed to happen," said Sittler.

MOST POINTS BY A DEFENSEMAN IN ONE SEASON

139: Bobby Orr, Boston Bruins, 1970–71

Bobby Orr revolutionized hockey with his rink-length dashes, creative playmaking and daring forays into the opponents' zone. (Prior to Orr, NHL defensemen focussed on defending and clearing the puck out of their own end; they rarely joined the rush—let alone led one.) With his rapid acceleration and open-ice artistry, the Bruins blueliner was the most electrifying talent the NHL had ever seen. As former NHLer turned TV commentator Bill Clement said about Orr: "He was such a package of grace and elegance that you would get caught watching him, then the horror would set in about what he was about to do to you." Until Orr's arrival, the single-season record for points by a defenseman was held by Pierre Pilote, with 59. Orr broke that standard by scoring 64 points in his third season, then upped the mark to an incredible 120 points the following year as he became the only rearguard to win an NHL scoring title. That season no other player reached 100 points. In 1970–71, the Bruins superstar added to his legend by extending the record to a staggering 139 points on 37 goals and 102 assists. And though Paul Coffey took a valiant run at Orr's record in 1985–86, he fell one point short, leaving this one looking like it could last forever.

3 games to none: Toronto Maple Leafs vs. Detroit Red Wings, 1942

3 games to none: New York Islanders vs. Pittsburgh Penguins, 1975

Faith plays a huge part in winning, especially in comebacks. That may be why only two playoff teams have ever had the never-say-die spirit to rebound from the most daunting challenge in league sports: a three-game deficit in a best-of-seven series. In 1975's quarterfinals against Pittsburgh, the New York Islanders faced almost insurmountable odds. It was only their third NHL season and they had but one round of playoff experience. Worse, during the first three matches, the Isles never once held the lead. Amazingly, their four-game comeback was completed in a showdown on road ice. As for Toronto's epic turnaround of 1942, it had the Stanley Cup at stake—no team in professional sports had blown three games and taken the next four to capture a championship series. The pivotal match was Game 4. After three losses to Detroit and a new strategy of dumping the puck in against Toronto's slow-footed defensemen, Leafs coach Hap Day benched two popular scoring stars and shamelessly read his team an impassioned letter from a young fan. What happened next was called a miracle. Toronto won a 4–3 pressure-cooker and triumphed in the next two matches to force a sudden-death seventh game—one that resulted in a 3–1 victory and a joyous night for Toronto's faithful.

MOST STANLEY CUPS WON BY A PLAYER

11: Henri Richard, 1956 to 1975

Henri Richard will forever skate in the shadow of his famous older brother, Maurice, except when this record is hauled out. The Pocket Rocket won an unsurpassed 11 Stanley Cups during his glorious 20-year tenure with the Montreal Canadiens. Amazingly, his personal stash of Cups outnumbers the totals of all but two teams in NHL history—the Canadiens' and the Toronto Maple Leafs'. Indeed, silver just seemed to follow the younger Richard around. His first five Cups came in his first five NHL seasons, when the Canadiens went on a championship spree between 1956 and 1960; surrounded by a wealth of talent, he subsequently never played more than four consecutive seasons without winning Lord Stanley's mug. In 180 postseason games, he collected 49 goals and 129 points, and two of those goals were Cup-winners: one in overtime of Game 6 against Detroit's Roger Crozier in 1966, the other in Game 7 against Chicago's Tony Esposito in 1971. When he retired in 1975, the fiery five-foot-seven centre had appeared in more playoff games than anyone in NHL history. The only other individual to equal the Pocket Rocket's 11 championships (as a player or coach) is Toe Blake, who copped three Cups as a player, and eight as Montreal's bench boss (between 1956 and 1968).

HIGHEST PERCENTAGE OF A TEAM'S OFFENSE IN A SEASON

57.3%: Mario Lemieux, Pittsburgh Penguins, 1988–89

Take a moment to properly absorb this number. It's really quite extraordinary. In 1988–89, Mario Lemieux enjoyed the most spectacular season of his career, cruising to the scoring title with 199 points on 85 goals and 114 assists—a whopping 31 points ahead of his closest pursuer, Wayne Gretzky. Making the maximum use of his strength, size and huge wingspan, the six-foot-four centre either scored or helped set up 57.3 per cent of the 347 goals the Penguins produced. This monumental effort broke the record of 52.7 per cent set by Joe Malone in 1919–20, and tied by Lemieux in 1987–88, when he racked up 168 points on Pittsburgh's 319 goals. At age 23, Lemieux had not even reached his prime, making one wonder what he might have achieved had his next five seasons not been interrupted by a litany of injuries, incuding back and hip ailments and a bout with Hodgkin's disease. Propelled by No. 66's brilliance, the long-slumbering Penguins won 40 games in 1988–89 and made the playoffs for the first time in seven years. Yet despite Lemieux's superhuman display, the voters awarded the Hart Trophy to Gretzky, who, after his headline-making trade from Edmonton, sparked the Los Angeles Kings to their best season since 1981.

MOST STANLEY CUPS WON BY A COACH

9: Scotty Bowman, 1967 to 2002

If hockey ever had an iceman, it was Scotty Bowman. "Cold" was the word Ken Dryden used to describe him. Pete Mahovlich called him an outright liar, one who won at all costs. Shawn Burr concluded his bench boss was retarded. And Dino Ciccarelli said: "He was a great coach and a rotten person." Of the 110 players who won a Stanley Cup with Bowman, few uttered anything complimentary—except on the day they received their championship rings, as Steve Shutt once observed. Bowman played mind games and was a master manipulator, keeping his players on edge, off-balance and intimidated. He picked out his whipping boys, such as Mahovlich and Slava Kozlov, and, in a departure from the style of his mentor Toe Blake, chastised them before their teammates and the press. But Bowman's methods worked. He won because his troops never got complacent. If anything, they trusted him behind the bench, where, with swelled chest and jutting jaw, he was always one step ahead of his players and a few up on opposing coaches. Meanwhile, most of his colleagues praised him grudgingly, perhaps jealously. After all, Bowman's record of 223 playoff wins well outnumbers the 209 total playoff games coached by his nearest rival, Al Arbour. The iceman captured a league-high nine Cups with a record three teams.

LONGEST CONSECUTIVE-GAMES POINT-SCORING STREAK

51 games: Wayne Gretzky, Edmonton Oilers,
October 5, 1983, to January 28, 1984

After being rudely swept in the 1983 Stanley Cup finals by the New York Islanders, the Edmonton Oilers opened 1983–84 on a mission, and, with their high-octane offense firing on all cylinders, laid waste to the league. Heading the attack was Wayne Gretzky, who began piling up points with abandon. By midseason, the Great One had notched a point in each of Edmonton's games and seemed bound to continue his torrid pace for the entire campaign. But his streak came to a jarring halt in Game 52, when the Oilers hosted the Los Angeles Kings (winless in their previous nine games). That night, Gretzky, nursing a shoulder injury, was blanked by unsung Finnish netminder Markus Mattsson in a 4–2 defeat. Coach Glen Sather kept his superstar on the ice for most of the last five minutes in a bid to keep the streak alive, but Gretzky's fourth and final shot—with two seconds left—was stopped by Mattsson, playing only his second game with the Kings since being recalled from the minors eight days before. During his 51-game streak, Gretzky scored 61 goals and 92 assists for a jaw-dropping 153 points. Including the last nine regular-season games of the previous year, the Oilers phenom had scored in 60 consecutive games.

MOST GOALS IN ONE SEASON

92: Wayne Gretzky, Edmonton Oilers, 1981–82

Wayne Gretzky's most famous "other" number is 92, though some would argue it should be 215. Or maybe 894. And even 50-in-39. But as stratospheric as these figures are, Gretzky's 92-goal mark may be his most impressive achievement. It has never been seriously threatened. In fact, it has only been approached by Gretzky himself (87 goals), Brett Hull (86) and Mario Lemieux (85). By today's standards, it would take the goal totals of two elite players to match what Gretzky did in 1981–82, when he destroyed Phil Esposito's 76-goal NHL mark by a 21 per cent margin and eclipsed his next-closest competitor's goal count, Mike Bossy's 64 goals, by 44 per cent. Even more remarkable, Gretzky bagged the 92-goal total in a mere 55 games. And he had 22 multiple-goal games where he scored 59 times—most often against Los Angeles' Mario Lessard, whom he victimized seven times, with an additional five each against Hartford's Greg Millen, Philadelphia's Pete Peeters and Calgary's Reggie Lemelin. To hit his famous 50 goals in 39 games, Gretzky scored in just 28 contests. Unlike Maurice Richard's history-making 50 goals in 1944–45, Gretzky's 92 is a record that is unlikely to ever be surpassed.

MOST CAREER PLAYOFF WINS BY A GOALIE

151: Patrick Roy, 1986 to 2003

Sacre Bleu! At his retirement, Patrick Roy had more playoff *wins* than any other goalie had *games played* in the postseason. His dominance was Gretzky-like, with 151 victories compared to Grant Fuhr's 150 games played. And though his total is largely a product of the glut of games in four-round playoff hockey, Roy was the ultimate pressure goalie. He could carry an entire team on his shoulders, as he did with championship results when he led Montreal to surprise Cups in 1986 and 1993, then later in Colorado, where he backstopped higher-calibre rosters to become that final-playoff puzzle piece for the Avalanche franchise. Physical skills aside, it was Roy's intensity and confidence that jacked his club to another level of play. His ego was certainly as big as his talent, but he backed up his cockiness with mental skills that made him practically indestructible through the rigors of the postseason. He had the ability to block out distractions and stay focussed. And technically, he was almost unbeatable, though he was outplayed on occasion. He lost his share of crucial Game 7s, for example, notably to Dallas and Detroit, and one final series against Calgary in 1989. No netminder has suffered more playoff losses. But that comes with winning, as Roy knows better than anyone.

MOST GOALS IN ONE GAME

7: Joe Malone, Quebec Bulldogs, January 31, 1920

Just how good was "Phantom" Joe Malone? It took Maurice Richard's legendary 50 goals in 50 games to top Malone's 44-goal count of 1917–18. But Malone did it in a 24-game schedule, which means, as prolific as Wayne Gretzky was, he never approached Phantom Joe's 2.20 goals-per-game average. As for Pavel Bure, when he struck 59 of Florida's 200 goals in 2000–01, he recorded modern hockey's highest percentage of team goals in one season: 29.5 per cent. Malone? In 1919–20, he had 39 of Quebec's 91 goals, for 42.9 per cent. Even so, Malone's greatest scoring achievement is still the seven goals he netted against the Toronto St. Pats in January 1920. With a reported temperature of –25°F outside, it was so cold in the small Quebec City arena that Toronto's Corbett Denneny quit the game because of a badly frozen hand and, unfortunately, few witnessed Malone's extraordinary night. The Phantom scored once in the first period and had hat tricks in the second and third frames of the Bulldogs' 10–6 win. In an effort to stop the deluge, the St. Pats switched goalies: Ivan Mitchell for Howie Lockhart. Even referee Cooper Smeaton tried thwarting Malone by disallowing one of his early goals. Today, Malone's super seven remains one of the game's indisputable milestones.

35 games: Philadelphia Flyers, October 14, 1979, to January 7, 1980

Most believed that the retirement of star goalie Bernie Parent meant Philadelphia was destined for tough times in 1979–80. Sensing the team was entering a transition phase, the Flyers' management removed the captaincy from Bobby Clarke and gave it to 24-year-old Mel Bridgman. And though a 9–2 loss to Atlanta in the Flyers' second game seemed ominous, after that rout, the club went on a remarkable roll. With coach Pat Quinn calling the shots and rookie Pete Peeters and journeyman Phil Myre sharing cage duties, the Flyers eclipsed the Montreal Canadiens' 28-game unbeaten streak by wasting Boston 5–2 on December 22, 1979, then extended the string to 35 games before being thumped 7–1 by the Minnesota North Stars on January 7, 1980. The defeat came at the end of a six-game road trip that saw the club play its last three games in four nights. Philadelphia logged 25 wins and 10 ties during the run, which ranks as the longest undefeated streak in North American pro sports, two more than the NBA's 1971–72 Los Angeles Lakers mark of 33 games. But the Flyers' record-setting surge led to no happy ending. Their season ended in bitterness when they were beaten by the New York Islanders on an overtime goal in Game 6 of the Cup finals.

MOST GOALS BY A ROOKIE IN ONE SEASON

76: Teemu Selanne, Winnipeg Jets, 1992–93

Although he was new to the North American game, Teemu Selanne had some advantages over other rookies when he joined the Winnipeg Jets in 1992. At 22, he was older and more experienced than most freshmen, having skated for Finland at the World Championships and at the Olympics. And too, the Jets had a strong core of European talent and played a freewheeling style that suited his game. Still, no one could have predicted what Selanne would accomplish. Blasting out of the gate, he scored 30 times in his first 38 games, and by late February, the Finnish Flash was closing in on Mike Bossy's NHL rookie record of 53 goals. On February 28, he blew past the 50-goal mark in dramatic style, scoring four times against Minnesota, then erased Bossy's mark in his next game with a hat trick against Quebec. As the season wore on, the turbocharged winger continued his torrid pace, ending the year with a 17-game point-scoring streak and an incredible 76 goals and 56 assists for 132 points. His 76 goals, the fifth-highest total in NHL history, tied Buffalo's Alexander Mogilny tally for the league lead, while his 132 points set a new rookie standard and broke Dale Hawerchuk's team record of 130 points. In all, Selanne shattered 14 Winnipeg scoring records.

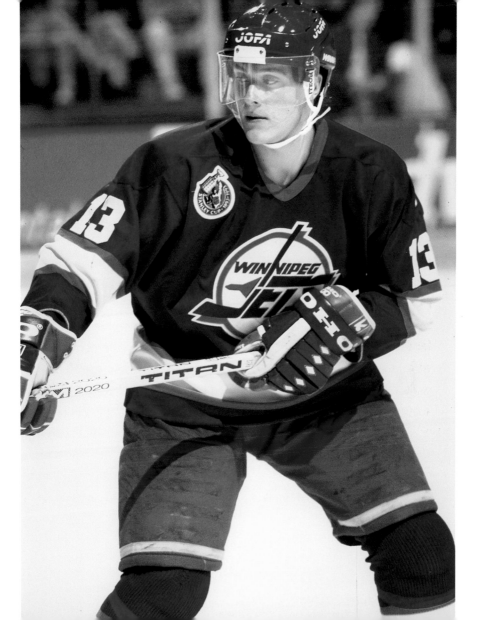

HIGHEST CAREER GOALS-PER-GAME AVERAGE

.762: Mike Bossy, New York Islanders, 1977–78 to 1986–87

"The Boss" was only the boss in name alone. Playing opposite Guy Lafleur and Wayne Gretzky during their peak years, Mike Bossy never commanded a scoring championship like he should have with his impressive numbers. In his best season of 147 points, he was still 65 behind Gretzky, which left him feeling disappointed and unappreciated. "It made it very insignificant as far as how good it was to me, and probably to a lot of people," Bossy once admitted to the *Hockey News*. So, to fulfill his aspirations for greatness, Bossy set his sights on the 50-goal benchmark, which was more than just a number to him. "I've let it become a personal gauge on whether I was successful or not. Probably because I've achieved it, I've let it become far too important for me," said Bossy. But that motivation drove him to an NHL-record nine consecutive 50-goal seasons and earned him a .762 goals-per-game average on 573 goals in 752 career games. It wasn't enough to top Gretzky's average of .838 during the 1980s nor Mario Lemieux's count of .823 after his first retirement. But Gretzky later slipped to .601 and, after returning to action once again in 2000–01, Lemieux's mark dropped to .754. Consequently, Bossy nabbed the record and, with it, a little more respect for his near-perfect career.

MOST CONSECUTIVE OVERTIME WINS
BY A GOALIE IN ONE PLAYOFF YEAR

10: Patrick Roy, Montreal Canadiens, 1993

Montreal's prospects did not look good early in the 1993 playoffs, after the club dropped the first two games of its series with the Quebec Nordiques. Patrick Roy surrendered a couple of soft goals, and Nords goaltending coach Dan Bouchard boasted that his team had solved the Canadiens netminder. But the rash remark backfired. Roy elevated his play, and the underdog Habs won 13 of their next 14 games, including seven in overtime, as they systematically disposed of the Nordiques, Buffalo Sabres and New York Islanders to advance to the finals against Wayne Gretzky and the Los Angeles Kings. The boys from Hollywood took the first game 4–1, but with the steely nerved Roy shutting the door, the Canadiens rebounded to win three pressure-packed overtime games in a row. The king of sudden-death had now extended his streak to an NHL-record 10 consecutive overtime victories. Back at the Montreal Forum for Game 5, the Canadiens then confidently cruised to a 4–1 triumph to claim the franchise's 24th Stanley Cup. Roy, who was dubbed "St. Patrick" by the media for his miraculous goaltending, compiled a sterling 2.13 goals-against average while winning 16 of 20 postseason games and claimed the Conn Smythe Trophy as MVP of the playoffs.

MOST SHUTOUTS BY A GOALIE IN ONE SEASON

22: George Hainsworth, Montreal Canadiens, 1928–29

George Hainsworth was given the unenviable task of replacing Georges Vezina in the Montreal net after the legendary goalie was fatally stricken with tuberculosis in 1925. But the tiny Torontonian, only five foot six and 150 pounds, proved himself a worthy successor, winning the newly created Vezina Trophy for fewest goals allowed in his first three seasons. In 1928–29, Hainsworth registered a phenomenal 22 shutouts and a microscopic goals-against average of 0.92 in a 44-game schedule, though there is no doubt the Habs goalie had some help in setting this record—most notably from the NHL rule book, which prohibited forward passing in the attacking zone. Given this advantage, teams found it easy to defend, and goalies benefited. Offense virtually disappeared in 1928–29; more than half of the games resulted in shutouts and only Boston managed to score an average of two goals per game, with last-place Chicago netting a paltry 33. Despite the dearth of scoring, however, Hainsworth still excelled; his 22 zeroes were nine more than any other goalie chalked up. The only team he failed to blank was Toronto. Interestingly, though the Canadiens had 22 wins in 1928–29, they did not win all of the 22 games in which Hainsworth posted a zero. Montreal was involved in six scoreless ties.

MOST GOALS IN A CAREER

894: Wayne Gretzky, 1979–80 to 1998–99

Few images in hockey are more familiar than that little dance Wayne Gretzky performed after scoring a goal. In one gliding motion, he'd kick his left foot high in the air and bring his right arm down, as if pulling a train whistle. The celebratory move was particularly well-known to goalies—at least the 155 Gretzky victimized during his 20-year career. Yet hockey's greatest marksman didn't have the hardest shot in the league, nor was he its fastest skater. And he was smallish by hockey standards. No, Gretzky's genius came from the way he saw the ice; he could anticipate plays as they developed better than anyone of his generation. He wore down his opponents by out-thinking them and forcing them to make decisions they hated. Goalies, in particular, detested Gretzky for the way he operated behind their nets in his so-called "office." From there, he would set up his slot man or dart out either way to make a pass or score on a wraparound. Defensemen also had trouble, because No. 99 could shoot and score against the grain, create open ice by daring blueliners to rush him and feed the puck to the trailing man on rushes. As one scout wrote: "Gretzky's backhand is as much of a threat as his forehand—for passes as well as shots." Gretzky claimed he never looked at the goalie; only the hole the goalie left open.

MOST CAREER GOAL-SCORING TITLES

7: Bobby Hull, Chicago Blackhawks, 1959–60 to 1968–69

Although Bobby Hull's much-publicized defection to the WHA's Winnipeg Jets prior to the 1972–73 season may have been a smart financial move (he signed a 10-year, $2.5-million contract), it cost him some valuable real estate in the NHL record books. At the time of his exit from the Chicago Blackhawks, Hull had compiled 604 goals, just 182 short of Gordie Howe's record total of 786, and he was still terrifying goalies with his booming slap shot. In fact, we can safely assume that all NHL goaltenders said a silent prayer of thanks when Hull took his brawn and his banana blade to the rival WHA. Had he not left, Hull likely would have overtaken Howe in the NHL's goal-scoring derby, particularly since scoring surged in the 1970s. The muscular left-winger would record 303 goals in seven WHA seasons in Winnipeg before returning to the NHL to conclude his career, netting six goals in a brief 27-game stint. Yet despite those missing WHA years, Hull still holds the NHL mark for most goal-scoring titles, with seven—one more than runner-up Phil Esposito. All of the Golden Jet's goal-scoring titles came in the 1960s, when he was hockey's most electrifying offensive force and a threat to score from anywhere inside the blue line.

FASTEST HAT TRICK BY A PLAYER

21 seconds: Bill Mosienko, Chicago Blackhawks, March 23, 1952

It was a nothing game. Both the hometown New York Rangers and the visiting Chicago Blackhawks had long been eliminated from the playoff race, so only 3,254 fans were on hand to witness Bill Mosienko's magic trick in the final game of the 1951–52 season. The fireworks erupted in the third period, with New York leading 6–2. Chicago's Gus Bodnar won a faceoff and passed the puck to Mosienko, who zipped around Rangers defenseman Hy Buller and snapped a low wrist shot past goalie Lorne Anderson, a rookie appearing in only his third NHL game. The goal came at 6:09. Chicago coach Ebbie Goodfellow left the line on the ice, and Bodnar again won the draw and directed a pass to Mosienko, who blew past Buller and fired the puck home at 6:20. There was then another faceoff and another win for Bodnar. This time, he passed to winger George Gee, who dashed down the ice and fed the puck to Mosienko. The speedy winger deked Anderson off his feet and lifted the biscuit into the twine at 6:30. Mosienko had scored three times in a rapid-fire 21 seconds. Incredibly, he remained on the ice and nearly netted a fourth goal a few seconds later. The stunned Rangers fell apart, losing 7–6, and Lorne Anderson never played in the NHL again.

LONGEST CONSECUTIVE-GAMES GOAL-SCORING STREAK

16 games: Harry "Punch" Broadbent, Ottawa Senators,
December 24, 1921, to February 15, 1922

Tough and talented, Punch Broadbent earned the nickname "Old Elbows" for his robust, physical style of play. A veteran of World War I, he served four years overseas with the RCAF, winning the Military Medal for heroism in combat. After the war, Broadbent then became an instrumental part of the great Ottawa Senators teams of the early 1920s. His offensive skills, hard hitting and dogged backchecking contributed significantly to the club's three Stanley Cup victories in 1920, 1921 and 1923, when he starred as the right-winger on one of hockey's top lines with Frank Nighbor and Cy Denneny. After staging a contract holdout for much of 1920–21, Broadbent produced his best offensive season in 1921–22, leading the loop in scoring with 32 goals and 46 points in a 24-game schedule. He notched 27 of the goals during a record 16 consecutive games, eclipsing Joe Malone's mark of 14. The streak began during a 10–0 rout of the Montreal Canadiens on December 24, and continued through to a 6–6 tie with the Canadiens on February 15. The closest modern-day challenger to Broadbent's long-standing milestone is Charlie Simmer, who counted goals in 13 straight games with the Los Angeles Kings in 1979–80.

AGE OF YOUNGEST SCORING CHAMPION

19 years, seven months: Sidney Crosby, Pittsburgh Penguins, 2006–07

The hockey world hasn't seen this kind of swagger in a kid since Wayne Gretzky lit up arenas around the NHL to capture his first scoring title at age 20 in 1980–81. Yet, as stunning as Gretzky's sophomore season was, Sidney Crosby beat the Great One to the Art Ross Trophy by eight months in 2006–07. Even more impressive, in the process, Crosby became the first teenage scoring champion in any major North American sports league, though Sid the Kid played nothing like a teenager. His 120-point season (36–84–120)—at age 19—challenged all athletic standards. Heck, it defied DNA, life's secret little building blocks. Crosby's double helix must have been encoded to skip the natural maturation process, ensuring he arrived fully loaded with great talent, passion, a drive for success and that second and third effort coaches call competitiveness. After notching his first six-point game on December 13, 2006, he took over the scoring lead for good, becoming the first teenager to do so since Gretzky battled for the title but lost it to Marcel Dionne in 1979–80. Then, on March 2, 2007, Crosby's goal against Carolina's Cam Ward made him the youngest player in league history to register 200 career points. The milestone came almost five months ahead of No. 99's 200th. No wonder Gretzky himself anointed Crosby "the Next One."

LONGEST SHUTOUT SEQUENCE BY A GOALIE (MODERN-DAY)

332:01: Brian Boucher, Phoenix Coyotes,
December 27, 2003, to January 11, 2004

Before Brian Boucher's stunning five-game shutout run of 2003–04, it would have been inconceivable that a nobody goalie on a go-nowhere team such as the Phoenix Coyotes could surpass Bill Durnan's famed 1949 modern-day shutout record of 309:21. While Durnan led the Montreal Canadiens to two Stanley Cups and topped the league with the best goals-against in *six* of eight years, Boucher's NHL career seemed to be over at the start of 2003–04. He was third on the depth chart behind Sean Burke and Zac Bierk and had been put on waivers—without a whiff of interest from the other 29 clubs. But when injuries opened up a spot in midseason, Boucher seized his opportunity. He blanked Los Angeles, Dallas, Carolina, Washington and Minnesota in an amazing display of more than five hours of shutout hockey before a deflected shot by Randy Robitaille snuck past him in a 1–1 tie against Atlanta. Many teams place messages on dressing-room walls as a motivation to players. But none is more famous than Montreal's "To you from failing hands" inscription, dedicated to past champions, including Durnan. Phoenix might consider taking some inspiration from Brian Boucher's dogged perseverence against the odds. How about: *Carpe diem?*

MOST CONSECUTIVE LEAGUE TITLES

7: Detroit Red Wings, 1948–49 to 1954–55

The Red Wings iced a series of strong teams during the 1940s, but in 1948–49, the Michigan club evolved into a powerhouse after coach Tommy Ivan created a new forward line by inserting veteran centre Sid Abel between a pair of dynamic young wingers named Gordie Howe and Ted Lindsay. Dubbed the Production Line, partly because they plied their trade in Detroit, the automotive capital of the U.S., but also because they produced an assembly-line stream of goals, assists and wins, the trio helped lead Detroit to top spot in the league. It was the opening salvo in a remarkable streak of seven straight first-place finishes for Detroit between 1948–49 and 1954–55. In 1949–50, the Production Line placed one-two-three in the scoring race, and the star-studded Red Wings won the Stanley Cup—a trophy they would claim again in 1952, 1954 and 1955. Seven consecutive NHL titles was not the only record that Detroit established during those dynasty years, either. In 1950–51, the Motor City mob gunned down the opposition, scoring an NHL-record 236 goals and amassing 101 points in the 70-game schedule to establish a standard that lasted 18 years, until Montreal collected 103 points in 76 games in 1968–69.

MOST CONSECUTIVE 50-GOAL SEASONS

9: Mike Bossy, New York Islanders, 1977–78 to 1985–86

Pro scouts doubted Mike Bossy's ability to make it in the NHL, claiming he was a timid player with too slight a frame to withstand the rigors of the big-league game. But the New York Islanders, who chose Bossy 15th overall in the 1977 Amateur Draft, knew he possessed an attribute that couldn't be taught—the ability to score. Skating on a line with Bryan Trottier and Clark Gillies, the whippet-lean winger scored 53 times in his freshman season, making him the first NHL rookie to crack the 50-goal plateau. He went on to break the barrier his first nine seasons—including 50 goals in his first 50 games in 1980–81, to tie Maurice Richard's 36-year-old record. Bossy equalled Richard's mark in dramatic style, too, connecting twice in the last five minutes of his 50th game. Producing in pressurized situations was typical of Bossy. As Islanders GM Bill Torrey noted, "A lot of the time, players look up at the clock and figure it's too late to score. It was never, never too late for Mike Bossy to score." If not for injury, Bossy would likely have extended his NHL record of nine straight 50-goal seasons. But chronic back pain caused him to miss 17 games in 1986–87 and he ended up with 38 goals. When the ailment did not respond to treatment, Bossy reluctantly retired at age 30.

MOST GOALS BY A TEAM IN ONE SEASON

446: Edmonton Oilers, 1983–84

Unleash the dogs. During the mid-1980s, Wayne Gretzky and his marauding pack of Oiler goalhounds not only defeated most of their opponents, they buried them. The Albertans topped the 400-goal plateau five times (a figure no other NHL team has ever reached)—highlighted by an NHL-record 446 goals in 1983–84, which translated into an NHL-record 1,182 scoring points. The offensive assault was nonstop. Four Oilers—Wayne Gretzky, Paul Coffey, Jari Kurri and Mark Messier—cracked the 100-point mark, while a fifth—Glenn Anderson—missed by one point. Playing like a man possessed, Gretzky paced the NHL scoring derby with 205 points and posted a point-scoring streak of 51 consecutive games. Hockey in the mid-1980s was played fast and loose, and the Oilers' heavy artillery blasted six or more goals in 40 games, exactly half of the 80-game schedule. A threat to score even when killing a penalty, Edmonton netted a record 36 shorthanded tallies, counted 10 or more goals in six separate thrashings and, during a bloodthirsty 11-game span in November, turned on the red light 84 times—an average of nearly eight goals per game. Considering all that firepower, it came as no great shock when the Oilers hoisted the Stanley Cup that spring.

34

MOST SHUTOUTS BY A ROOKIE GOALIE IN ONE SEASON

15: Tony Esposito, Chicago Blackhawks, 1969–70

To call Tony Esposito's rookie season impressive is an understatement—
he dominated. And no one saw it coming. Montreal, which lost Esposito to Chicago in the 1969 Interleague Draft, had not been impressed
with Esposito's unorthodox, scrambling, butterfly style. Even Chicago's management didn't expect Esposito to serve as much more than
a solid backup for veteran Denis DeJordy. Instead, Esposito surprised
everyone by winning the starter's job. On October 25, he registered his
first shutout of the season, beating the Canadiens 5–0 at the Montreal
Forum. He blanked his former team 1–0 in their next meeting three
weeks later; and by then he was stonewalling other teams, too. In fact,
"Tony O" went on to notch zeroes against every NHL team except the
Minnesota North Stars and the New York Rangers. His 38–17–8 record
and 2.17 goals-against average also led Chicago to first place, and he
won the Vezina and Calder trophies and was voted a First-Team All-
Star. Esposito would have captured the Hart Trophy as well if not for
the incomparable Bobby Orr, who became the first defenseman in NHL
history to win the scoring title. Esposito's mark of 15 shutouts, set in an
era of offensive hockey, has not been equalled since—and may never be,
much less by a rookie.

LARGEST MARGIN OF VICTORY
IN THE REGULAR-SEASON GOAL-SCORING RACE

35 goals: Brett Hull, St. Louis Blues, 1990–91

At his peak, Brett Hull was an unstoppable goal-scoring machine. In 1989–90 and 1990–91, he amassed goals in a higher percentage of games than either Wayne Gretzky or Mario Lemieux in their best back-to-back years, potting goals in 124 of the Blues' 183 games—including playoffs—for a 67.8 scoring percentage. Gretzky scored in 65.2 per cent of the Oilers' games (118 of 181 contests) in 1981–82 and 1982–83; Lemieux managed a high of 61.6 per cent (101 of 164) for Pittsburgh in 1987–88 and 1988–89. Hull's set-up man was centre Adam Oates. Each had talent, but together, it was lightning on ice. The Hull–Oates duo challenged the age-old strategy of playing a left-handed centre with a right-handed right-winger, a combo that meant the set-up man could feed the scorer with forehand passes. The tactic clicked for Bryan Trottier and Mike Bossy and later for Gretzky and Jari Kurri, but Hull and Oates bucked the trend. Both shot right. Yet Oates's exceptional passing skills and unselfish play gave Hull every advantage to fire off his powerful and accurate blast, which he could do from anywhere in a flash. In 1990–91, he netted 86 goals to Steve Yzerman, Cam Neely and Theoren Fleury's 51. It remains the greatest goal margin of victory in league history.

36

MOST POINTS IN ONE PLAYOFF YEAR

47: Wayne Gretzky, Edmonton Oilers, 1985

During his career, Wayne Gretzky accumulated 40 or more points in three postseasons—pretty amazing considering that Mario Lemieux is the only other player to reach that plateau, and he did it only once. Maybe the scariest aspect to this record is that the Edmonton Oilers played just 18 games in their relentless march to the 1985 Stanley Cup. Showcasing his fabled killer instinct, Gretzky collected 47 points on 17 goals and 30 assists, for an average of 2.6 points per game. If the Oilers had been forced to play more games, who knows how many points No. 99 might have put on the board. The Great One racked up points against all of Edmonton's opponents in the 1985 playoffs (Los Angeles, Winnipeg, Chicago and Philadelphia), but he inflicted the most serious damage on the Blackhawks, posting 18 points in six games as the Oilers set a single-series NHL record of 44 goals. The main benefactor of Gretzky's playmaking wizardry was linemate Jari Kurri, who scorched Chicago with 12 goals and three hat tricks. Then in the finals against the Flyers, Gretzky turned sniper, scoring seven times to equal the modern-day record (held by Jean Béliveau and Mike Bossy) for most goals in a finals as he paced the Oilers to a five-game triumph.

MOST GOALS SCORED IN DIFFERENT WAYS IN ONE GAME

5: Mario Lemieux, Pittsburgh Penguins, December 31, 1988

Mario Lemieux celebrated New Year's Eve in 1988 by doing something no other NHLer had ever done—score in every possible way a player can score; at even strength, on a power play, shorthanded, on a penalty shot and into an empty net. The dazzling display began when Lemieux netted an even-strength goal at 4:17 of the first period against New Jersey Devils goaltender Bob Sauve. His second goal, scored three minutes later while his team was killing a penalty, gave Pittsburgh a 2–1 lead. He then counted his third on a power play at 10:59, putting his club up 3–2. And at 11:14 of the second period, the Pens captain scored his fourth, beating relief goalie Chris Terreri on a penalty shot to give the Penguins a 6–4 lead. Finally, with just one second left in the game and Pittsburgh protecting a 7–6 lead, Lemieux scored into an empty net to cap an 8–6 victory. In the process of managing this historic feat, he became the first Penguins player to score five goals in a game. To top it off, he added three assists for an eight-point night. "Some of the things he did out there were amazing," said linemate Rob Brown. "He put the puck through his legs, he made some twirls. It was a classic example of the best hockey player in the world."

LONGEST CONSECUTIVE-GAMES POINT-SCORING
STREAK IN THE PLAYOFFS

27 games: Bryan Trottier, New York Islanders, 1980, 1981, 1982

There was nothing flashy about Bryan Trottier's game, but few forwards have ever been so effective at both ends of the ice. Sound defensively and blessed with keen offensive instincts, he was the NHL's elite centre until Wayne Gretzky's arrival. Raised on a cattle farm in the tiny Saskatchewan town of Val Marie, Trottier joined the Islanders straight from junior at age 19 in 1975–76 and quickly proved his mettle, winning the Calder Trophy as the NHL's outstanding rookie. His line, with Mike Bossy (a pure shooter, on the right) and Clark Gillies (a hulking grinder who ruled the corners, on the left), soon became the league's dominant offensive trio. In 1978–79, Trottier enjoyed the best campaign of his career, collecting 134 points and winning the Hart Trophy as MVP, though the first-place Isles stumbled in the playoffs and lost to the Rangers. Next season the club avenged that setback, capturing the first of four straight Stanley Cups, with Trottier, a key contributor, leading all playoff scorers in 1980 and 1982. In a remarkable display of consistency, he would tally points in 27 consecutive games over three postseasons, including 18 straight in 1981, setting the NHL mark for a playoff year. All told, Trottier amassed 42 points on 16 goals and 26 assists during the streak.

MOST CONSECUTIVE GAMES SCORING
A GOAL FROM THE START OF A CAREER

6: Evgeni Malkin, Pittsburgh Penguins, 2006–07

Evgeni Malkin's remarkable NHL start not only belongs among the league's greatest records, but, considering that none of hockey's most prolific scorers ever generated such consistency in their first half-dozen games, Malkin's six-game rookie run qualifies as an all-time top contender. When it was revealed that no freshman had accomplished the milestone in 89 years, Malkin was classed alongside legendary pioneers Joe Malone, Newsy Lalonde and Cy Denneny, who each scored in their first six NHL matches. Yet as different as these players' hockey eras were from Malkin's, so too was their status as first-year players. They played their eras' old-time 60-minutes-per-game style as rookies, but only because the league was in its own rookie year. As one scribe reflected, "The mere fact that the NHL was newly formed should not make a 10-year veteran like Joe Malone a rookie." Compared to the 20-year-old Russian, Malone was 27, Lalonde, 29, and Denneny, 25. Malkin skated into the record books on November 1, 2006, when teammate Sidney Crosby scooped up a loose puck and relayed it to Malkin, who caught Los Angeles goalie Dan Cloutier moving the wrong way and scored with a wrist shot from about 10 feet out at 8:29 of the opening period.

MOST WINS BY A ROOKIE GOALIE IN ONE SEASON

44: Terry Sawchuk, Detroit, 1950–51

Imagine finding a goalie who, in his first season, steals the coveted start-ing job from your defending Stanley Cup-winning netminder, estab-lishes a league-record number of shutouts, has a goals-against average of under 2.00, almost wins the Vezina Trophy as top goalie and lands on the First All-Star team. Throw in a Calder Trophy as best freshman and that is how Terry Sawchuk began his NHL career. The 1950–51 rookie award was his third in a row (he won rookie-of-the-year honours with Omaha in the USHL in 1947–48 and with the AHL Indianapolis Capitals in 1948–49). Sawchuk's trademark deep crouch was unorthodox, but it allowed him to remain on his feet for screened shots and loose pucks in goalmouth scrambles. The Winnipeg-born netminder played all 70 scheduled games to hand the Red Wings 44 wins and 101 points, both NHL records, and finished just one goal shy of winning the Vezina Tro-phy—which, at the time, was based on fewest goals. (The trophy went to Toronto's Al Rollins, who had played 30 fewer games.) As compensation for losing so narrowly, Detroit awarded Sawchuk a $1,000 bonus, the same sum given to Vezina winners by the league. Within a season, Saw-chuk would be regarded as one of the game's great netminders.

MOST CAREER OVERTIME GOALS IN THE PLAYOFFS

7: Joe Sakic, Colorado Avalanche, 1988–89 to 2006–07

On any given night, there weren't many players who could haul down Maurice Richard. Though during his days as hockey's purest goal scorer, Richard carried more than defenders on his back into scoring territory. He also bore the weight of his Canadiens, who won eight Stanley Cups off Richard's record six playoff overtime markers, including an unprecedented three in finals series action. In fact, the only place where the Rocket yielded was in the record books. And he didn't give in easily. A span of 48 years would pass before Joe Sakic wrestled away Richard's career mark—in a struggle that began in 1996—by scoring twice during Colorado's first Cup campaign. Sakic followed up by notching an overtime goal in 1998, two more in 2001 and another in 2004, to equal Richard's record. The record-setting seventh tally came via a tip-in off a John-Michael Liles slap shot, which snuck past Dallas goalie Marty Turco at 4:36 of the extra period to give Colorado a 5–4 victory on April 24, 2006. "I didn't do much," said Sakic, in his characteristically low-key manner. "I was just trying to get a screen in there. He shot it, and it just went off my stick." No, Joe, it was a much bigger goal, one that hockey had in its sights for almost a half-century.

MOST TOP 10 SCORERS FROM ONE TEAM

7: Boston Bruins, 1970–71

The Boston Bruins brought a new blend of blitzkrieg offense and smash-mouth hockey to the NHL in the late 1960s, one that vaulted them into the league's upper echelon. And, in the tight confines of boisterous Boston Garden, the Bruins' buzzsaw attack gave visiting teams nightmares. In 1969–70, Boston scored 277 goals en route to capturing the Stanley Cup. But the next season, with rookie coach Tom Johnson overseeing line changes, the Beantowners found another gear and began steam-rolling opponents with disdain, racking up an NHL-record 57 victories, 121 points and 399 goals—a startling 108 goals more than the tally of their closest rival, the Montreal Canadiens. Led by a devastating power play, the club boasted four 100-point scorers (in a league that had never seen a 100-point scorer prior to 1968–69), and seven of the circuit's top 10 point-getters—a feat not achieved before or since. The seven snipers included Phil Esposito, Bobby Orr, Johnny Bucyk, Ken Hodge, Wayne Cashman, Johnny McKenzie and Fred Stanfield. But all that amped up offense failed to win the swaggering Bruins a single playoff series. They were upset in the 1971 quarterfinals by Montreal and rookie goaltender Ken Dryden, who entered the playoffs with a grand total of six games of NHL experience.

GREATEST THIRD-PERIOD COMEBACK IN A PLAYOFF GAME

5 goals: Los Angels Kings vs. Edmonton Oilers, April 10, 1982

Few NHL games have merited a nickname more than the Los Angeles–Edmonton divisional clash in 1982, the fabled "Miracle on Manchester." The tortoise-versus-hare matchup pitted the season's worst postseason qualifier, the pitiful 24–41–15 Kings, against the powerful Oilers, who, after rewriting the record books with the most feared and potent offense in NHL history, were overwhelming favourites. They were young, brash and held a record-setting 48-point regular-season differential on their California opponents. In other words, Edmonton was ripe for an ambush. Game 3 tipped the scales at the Great Western Forum on Manchester Boulevard in Los Angeles. Edmonton commanded a 5–0 lead after two periods, but instead of playing defensively, the Oilers stuck with their typical, wide-open style. What happened in the next 20 minutes, and, then, in overtime, will go down in playoff history as the greatest single-game comeback ever. The Kings clawed their way back by scoring five unanswered goals, forcing overtime on a goal by Steve Bozek with only five seconds remaining, then winning the game on a back-breaker from rookie Daryl Evans at 2:25 of sudden death. Amid the deafening roar from the crowd, the Oilers stood in disbelief, watching as the Kings celebrated.

MOST CONSECUTIVE PLAYOFF-SERIES WINS BY A TEAM

19: New York Islanders, 1980 to 1984

After the New York Islanders swept the Edmonton Oilers in the 1983 finals to capture a fourth straight Stanley Cup, GM Bill Torrey noted, "Our guys are never satisfied. Who knows how long they'll keep it up?" Torrey was never satisfied either. He constantly juggled his roster, adding key role players to build and maintain a team with a formidable blend of skill and grit. In addition to superstars Denis Potvin, Bryan Trottier and Mike Bossy, the Isles boasted a platoon of hard-hitting foot soldiers headed by Clark Gillies, Bob Nystrom, John Tonelli, Butch Goring and Brent and Duane Sutter, plus a money goaltender in Billy Smith. En route to winning the 1983 Cup, New York extended its skein of playoff series victories to 16, eclipsing the NHL record of 13 set by Montreal in the 1970s. The Isles then won three more series in the 1984 playoffs, bringing their mark to 19 consecutive series wins. But by the time they reached the finals, Al Arbour's injury-riddled warriors had no answer for a young and hungry Edmonton crew. After the teams split the first two games, the Oilers' offense clicked into high gear and Edmonton stormed to victory, outscoring the Isles 19–6 in the next three contests to take the Cup.

MOST SAVES BY A GOALIE IN ONE PLAYOFF YEAR

761: *Kirk McLean, Vancouver Canucks, 1994*

Kirk McLean's heroics between the pipes in the 1994 playoffs are often overlooked in the discussion of great postseason feats. This is a real injustice, considering the 27-year-old puckstopper carried the overachieving Canucks to within one game of taking the Stanley Cup while facing the heaviest barrage of rubber in playoff annals. McLean was especially sharp against Calgary in the first round, when the Canucks won three straight overtime tilts to take the series in seven games, and in the finals against the heavily favoured New York Rangers, when he stole Game 1 in Manhattan with a sensational 52-save performance, including 17 in overtime. In 24 playoff matches in 1994, McLean stopped 761 of 820 shots. Both totals are playoff records by wide margins. In fact, no other NHL goaltender has made even 700 saves in one postseason. Captain Kirk faced an average of 34 shots per game and posted a .928 save percentage despite a withering travel schedule that saw Vancouver crisscross the continent, playing four, tough series in Calgary, Dallas, Toronto and New York. Yet despite McLean's sublime effort, his team lost 3–2 in Game 7 of the finals, and Rangers defenseman Brian Leetch was awarded the Conn Smythe Trophy as playoff MVP.

MOST GOALS IN ONE PLAYOFF YEAR

19: Reggie Leach, Philadelphia Flyers, 1976
19: Jari Kurri, Edmonton Oilers, 1985

Some hockey fans may find it surprising that Reggie Leach and Jari Kurri share this prestigious playoff record. After all, neither winger was considered the most talented player on his team and their names do not exactly litter the record books. But there is no arguing with their achievement. Leach's 19 goals in 16 postseason games in 1976 broke a record that had stood for 57 years—Newsy Lalonde's 17 goals in 1919. And the Manitoban managed to do it even though his team did not win the Stanley Cup. Incredibly, both players reached the record with little help from the power play. Leach notched just two of his 19 goals on the man-advantage; Kurri, only one. But by all rights, Kurri should have surpassed Leach. The Finnish sharpshooter scored 18 goals in Edmonton's first 13 playoff games in 1985 and entered the finals needing only two more to establish a new standard. But as fate would have it, in the finals the Oilers met Leach's former team, the Flyers, and they were not in a mood to co-operate. Even though Edmonton racked up 21 goals, rolling over the injury-plagued Flyers in five games, the closely checked Kurri scored only once—and that came in an 8–3 blowout in the last game of the series.

47

MOST SHOTS ON GOAL IN ONE SEASON

550: Phil Esposito, Boston Bruins, 1970–71

Despite establishing numerous marks during the early 1970s, there is little evidence remaining in the record books of Boston's domination in enemy territory. Much of the Bruins' hard work was smashed by Montreal and Edmonton's dynasty teams, but Phil Esposito's shots record is one of the exceptions. The so-called Sultan of Slot, Esposito was a trigger-happy freight train who terrorized goalies and defensemen in vicious battles for puck control and elbow room on the crease's doorstep. Of course, he was also tagged a "garbage collector" because of his uncanny knack for picking up cheap goals on tip-ins and rebounds and in ugly goalmouth scrambles. But the salvos didn't bother Esposito, who fired back in *Sports Illustrated:* "I don't care if the puck goes in off my head." In fact, a few did. His scoring touch was unorthodox and unique, and no player potted as many goals squarely in front of the net. He turned the slot into his office—a personal war zone for his quick-release snap shot that, next to the corners, was the toughest place to play abuse-wise. In his eighth NHL season, Esposito scored 76 times while blasting an all-time-high 550 shots, a steady stream of seven per game. No NHLer has come within 120 shots of matching Esposito's feat.

48

MOST GOALS BY A DEFENSEMAN IN ONE GAME

5: Ian Turnbull, Toronto Maple Leafs, February 2, 1977

Ian Turnbull's name is not prominent in the NHL record books. In fact, he is limited to just one entry. But neither Paul Coffey, Denis Potvin, Ray Bourque or any other marquee defenseman has matched Turnbull's feat of potting five goals in a game. The outburst came in a 9–1 pasting of Detroit on Groundhog Day in 1977. Turnbull would set a Leafs record of 22 goals by a defenseman in 1976–77 (tied by Al Iafrate in 1987–88), though he came into the contest mired in a terrible slump, having scored only twice in his previous 35 games. "It was just one of those nights when everything goes in," Turnbull said later. "I wish the track had been going this afternoon. I probably would have cleaned up." Turnbull netted his first two goals against goalie Ed Giacomin, who was replaced at the start of the third period by Jim Rutherford. Turnbull then scored on Rutherford to notch the first hat trick of his career at 4:58, but didn't connect again until the 17:10 mark, when Stan Weir's high, floating pass deflected in off his arm. His fifth goal, at 18:30, was the product of a planned play: Borje Salming hit his streaking defensive partner with a perfect pass that sent Turnbull in on a breakaway; he then coolly beat Rutherford with a low shot to bag the record.

MOST POWER-PLAY GOALS IN ONE SEASON

34: Tim Kerr, Philadelphia Flyers, 1985–86

Tim Kerr was nicknamed "the Slot Machine," a tribute to his deadly scoring efficiency from the area between the faceoff circles. A huge man at six foot three and 230 pounds, he was nearly impossible to budge when parked in front of the opposition net. And in 1983–84, banging in rebounds and deflecting point shots, he recorded his first of four consecutive 50-goal seasons to become one of the league's most feared forwards and the linchpin of the Flyers' power play. In 1985–86, he counted 58 goals, including an NHL record 34 with the man-advantage. He followed that with another 58-goal effort the next season and again led the league with 26 power-play tallies. Unfortunately, the rest of Kerr's career was marred by injuries, including most of the 1987–88 season when he underwent five shoulder operations. Though he rebounded to net 48 goals in 1988–89, more injuries followed and his play went into decline. Tragedy also struck his personal life, when, in October 1990, his wife died just 10 days after the birth of the couple's baby. Today, Kerr is director of Tim Kerr Charities. The non-profit group's work includes "Powerplay for Life," a program that raises money for charity every time the Flyers score Kerr's former specialty—a power-play goal.

MOST SAVES BY A GOALIE IN A PLAYOFF GAME

113: Tiny Thompson, Boston Bruins, April 3–4, 1933

Tiny Thompson's stunning performance against Toronto during the 1933 playoffs has mysteriously vanished from history's radar screen. This may be because it happened so long ago, but also because Thompson was the losing goalie. In retrospect, it's not surprising that this 1933 play-off game went into overtime—three of the previous four clashes in the best-of-five semifinals were decided in sudden death. But Game 5 was a hellish grind. With Thompson and Leafs goalie Lorne Chabot stubbornly turning aside every puck fired their way, the two clubs struggled through 164 minutes and 46 seconds of scoreless hockey. In fact, the teams were so bone-weary after playing eight periods that they were going to toss a coin to decide the winner. The players were lined up at centre ice awaiting the coin flip, when Bruins coach Art Ross changed his mind and suggested playing the ninth period with no goalies. But the netminders voted against it, so back the teams went. Finally, at 1:48 a.m., Toronto forward Ken Doraty, the smallest player on the ice at 133 pounds, whipped a shot home to end the game and the series. Thompson finished the marathon with 113 saves on 114 shots, while Chabot blocked 93 to set his own NHL record: most saves in a shutout.

51

MOST PENALTY MINUTES IN A CAREER

3,966: Tiger Williams, 1974–75 to 1987–88

Dave Williams was called a lot of things during his riotous career, but he never disguised his intentions or pretended to be anything other than what he was. He picked up the nickname "Tiger" playing goalie at age six, when, if his team wasn't winning, he'd stickhandle the puck up-ice and try to score. He came from a family of fighters; his brothers were all provincial boxing champions in Saskatchewan. But Williams played hockey with more than just a numb skull and knuckles. Quick with a quip (he once famously announced that the Penguins were "done like dinner"), Williams could score with relative consistency, and he stayed mentally strong, too. In 14 seasons, he elbowed, cross-checked, speared, whacked and punched his way to a league-record 3,966 minutes—the equivalent of 66 full games of incarceration. Most tough guys don't stay tough for so long or get as philosophical. If such a thing exists, Williams was the thinking-man's goon. He considered fighting, or as he termed it, "the challenge of gaining an advantage," as a way to create momentum. And he called himself an anarchist, one whose only obligation on-ice was to help his guys win. His live-by-the-sword philosophy served him well when he retired, too. He never whined or apologized for the way he had played.

MOST POINTS BY A TEAM IN ONE SEASON

132: Montreal Canadiens, 1976–77

The Canadiens won four straight Stanley Cups between 1976 and 1979, and, while the core of the team remained consistent during the four-year run, the 1976–77 edition was likely the best of the bunch. Blessed with size and speed and deep at all positions, the Habs rolled to a 60–8–12 mark for an NHL-record 132 points, while suffering just one defeat on home ice. Miles ahead of everyone else in the standings, Montreal actually played better as the season wore on, losing only once in its last 34 games. Guy Lafleur copped the scoring title with 136 points and the Hart Trophy as MVP, Steve Shutt led the league with 60 goals, Larry Robinson won the Norris Trophy as best defenseman and goalies Ken Dryden and Bunny Larocque shared the Vezina Trophy. Montreal scored 387 goals while allowing only 171 for a plus-differential of 216, the highest of any team in NHL annals. Oh yeah, and the coach was the one and only Scotty Bowman, a hard-driving perfectionist who refused to allow his elite troops to lapse into complacency. As expected, the Canadiens' juggernaut captured the Cup in 1977, and managed it without much difficulty, losing only two postseason games and sweeping two of its three series.

53

MOST WINS BY A TEAM IN ONE SEASON

62: *Detroit Red Wings, 1995–96*

Detroit went from a good team to a great one in 1995–96 by bucking conventional wisdom and playing all five of their Russian players—Igor Larionov, Sergei Fedorov, Slava Kozlov, Viacheslav Fetisov and Vladimir Konstantinov—as a unit for much of the season. Other NHL teams avoided putting all their European imports together, but the quintet's old-time Soviet finesse game was a perfect complement to Steve Yzerman, Paul Coffey, Nicklas Lidstrom and the rest of Detroit's talented roster. The Russified Red Wings romped to the President's Trophy with a 62–13–7 record and 131 points—a stunning 27 more than their nearest rival, the Colorado Avalanche, could boast. Deadly at home, Detroit also went 36–3–2 at Joe Louis Arena to tie the 1975–76 Philadelphia Flyers' record for most home wins in a season. And though the Wings finished one point shy of the 1976–77 Montreal Canadiens' NHL record of 132 points, the club surpassed the Habs' record 60-win total by two, albeit aided by a schedule two games longer than Montreal's. The common denominator between the two teams: coach Scotty Bowman, who pushed the Wings hard to break his former team's mark. But Bowman may have pushed too hard. Motown's record-setting season lost much of its lustre when Colorado eliminated Detroit in the Conference finals.

54

MOST CONSECUTIVE GAMES PLAYED
IN A CAREER (INCLUDING PLAYOFFS)

949: Garry Unger, February 24, 1968, to December 22, 1979

When Atlanta coach Al MacNeil benched Garry Unger on December 22, 1979, he not only ended Unger's record-setting regular-season streak at 914 games, but probably cost him the all-time ironman mark as well. That's because Unger stayed healthy during the rest of 1979–80 to play another consecutive 52 games, which would cap him at 967 (including that fateful missed game). Eight years later, Doug Jarvis would claim the regular-season title with 964 straight matches, or three *less* than Unger's fantasy total had he not been benched. It wasn't like MacNeil didn't have a choice, either. Unger was dressed with a slight shoulder injury. The Flames were winning comfortably, 7–3 against the Blues, Unger's former team, and the crowd at St. Louis's Checkerdome was chanting "Garry, Garry, Garry," urging MacNeil to play its one-time captain. Even a few of Unger's teammates made an appeal, but Mac-Neil refused to let Unger take a shift, declaring, "I run the club, not you guys." Still, Unger never missed a playoff tilt during his 11-year string of 914 regular-season and 35 playoff games. Jarvis, on the other hand, sat out four playoff matches in 1979, interrupting his run at 362 games when the postseason is included.

MOST SAVES BY A GOALIE IN A REGULAR-SEASON GAME

80: Sam LoPresti, Chicago Blackhawks, March 4, 1941

Sam LoPresti, a rookie from Eveleth, Minnesota, playing in only his 23rd NHL game, stepped into a shooting gallery at Boston Garden in this 1941 tilt. The Bruins fired 27 shots on Chicago's net in the first period, 33 in the second and 23 in the third. And LoPresti stopped 42 of them before Roy Conacher scored in the second frame to tie the game 1–1. Milt Schmidt connected on the Bruins' 58th shot late in the period, but the Hawks knotted the game in the third and LoPresti still had a chance for the win until Eddie Wiseman beat him from close in with two minutes left. Despite the loss, LoPresti turned aside 80 of the 83 missiles directed his way. Bruins goalie Frank Brimsek, who was also from Eveleth, had a far easier night, facing only 20 shots. Asked later whether LoPresti had been good or lucky, Boston's Johnny Crawford stated, "He was good alright. If he hadn't been good he wouldn't be alive now." Still, surviving the Boston onslaught was nothing compared to what Lopresti endured after he left the NHL to serve in World War II. He was aboard a U.S. merchant ship in 1943 that was torpedoed by a German U-boat off the coast of Africa. LoPresti and 20 crewmates spent 42 days floating in a lifeboat before being rescued by a passing freighter.

MOST GOALS IN ONE PLAYOFF SERIES

12: Jari Kurri, Edmonton Oilers, 1985

If any player was underrated because he played in the shadow of a famous teammate, it was Wayne Gretzky's magical right-winger Jari Kurri. An extraordinary marksman and superb defensive forward, Kurri was arguably the most complete player on the shoot-it-out champion Oilers teams of the 1980s. With blinding speed and skill to burn, his two-way finesse game could beat an opponent any way. He also read teammates and opponents so accurately that he became a central figure in Edmonton's evolution to "play well for 200 feet of ice in every part of the game," as Gretzky once put it. In each of Edmonton's four Stanley Cups with No. 99, Kurri led all playoff goal scorers. And during their 1985 assault on Lord Stanley, the Oilers loaded up their playoff-series record of 44 goals on the 12 tallies that Kurri notched against Chicago in the Conference finals. The six-game series saw a record 69 goals scored, while the Finn set a new mark of three hat tricks, the last two coming in consecutive games to tie Doug Bentley's 1944 playoff record. Kurri connected twice in Game 1, three times in Game 2, three times in Game 5 and four times in Game 6 to break Newsy Lalonde's 1919 record of 11 goals in a playoff series. Remarkably, Gretzky's sidekick reached his record total with only one power-play marker.

LONGEST UNBEATEN STREAK BY A GOALIE

32 games: Gerry Cheevers, Boston Bruins, 1971–72

The concept of the decorated goalie mask began in the late 1960s, when Gerry Cheevers began painting black stitches on his white mask each time it was dinged by a puck or stick. The garish markings soon became his trademark. But Cheevers's contributions went far beyond arty gimmicks. He may not have put up flashy shutout or goals-against numbers, but no one was better at making clutch saves. As he put it, "I don't care much about my average. My philosophy has always been that the other team can fill the net on me as long as we get one more goal." In 1971–72, Cheevers and Ed Johnston split the netminding as the Bruins roared to a 54-win season. Both won 27 games, but Cheevers's total included a 32-game unbeaten streak that obliterated Frank Brimsek's record of 23 games, set in 1940–41. Cheevers capped his season by backstopping Boston to the Stanley Cup. Many great goalies have come and gone since 1971–72, but Cheevers's record has never been topped—and only one goalie has come close. In 1982–83, Pete Peeters had a banner year with Boston, winning 40 games and compiling a 31-game unbeaten streak. Peeters credited much of his success to his coach, for creating a relaxed atmosphere in which he could thrive. His coach was none other than Gerry Cheevers.

AGE OF OLDEST SCORING CHAMPION

36 years, five months: Bill Cook, New York Rangers, 1932–33
Considering Gordie Howe's longevity, there aren't many greybeard records he doesn't own. But surprisingly, he is not the NHL's oldest scoring champion. When he won his last Art Ross Trophy at age 34, Howe was still 18 months younger than Bill Cook, who earned the scoring title at age 36 in 1932–33. Cook, who came out of the old western pro leagues, played for Saskatoon before joining the expansion New York Rangers in 1926–27. He was the first player signed by the club, its first captain and the first Ranger to score an NHL goal. New York built its franchise around the 30-year-old newcomer, who was teamed with his brother Bun Cook and Frank Boucher to form the famed A Line. The line's precision passing decimated opposing defenses, and Cook won the scoring title in his first NHL season. The next year, the Rangers captured their first Stanley Cup, with every one of the club's goals in the final series against the Montreal Maroons coming off the blades of the A Line. The unit stayed together for several more seasons, earning the then-36-year-old Cook his second scoring championship, on 28 goals and 50 points, in 1932–33. Cook capped off the year by pocketing the NHL's first overtime Cup-winning goal.

LONGEST TEAM WINNING-STREAK

17 games: Pittsburgh Penguins, March 9 to April 10, 1993

Pittsburgh's hopes of winning a third straight Stanley Cup suffered a serious blow in early January 1993, when Mario Lemieux, who had registered a blistering 103 points in his first 40 games, aggravated an old back injury. While the NHL's leading scorer was sidelined, doctors removed a lump from his neck and performed a biopsy that revealed the early stages of Hodgkin's disease, a form of lymphatic cancer. Lemieux missed 24 games while undergoing a draining series of radiation treatments. Yet incredibly, on March 2, the day of his last treatment, Lemieux played against Philadelphia, notching a goal and an assist and earning a standing ovation from Flyers fans. With their big gun back in the fold, the inspired Penguins then went on a tear, logging an NHL-record 17 straight victories, while in the 20 games after his return from sick bay, Lemieux posted an astounding 57 points to complete one of the greatest individual comebacks in sports history. The offensive binge, which included back-to-back four-goal games and one five-goal game, enabled him to overtake Buffalo's Pat LaFontaine to claim the scoring title by 12 points. Unfortunately, Lemieux's back problems flared up in the division finals, and the defending champions were upset by the New York Islanders.

60

AGE OF OLDEST NHL PLAYER

52 years, 11 days: Gordie Howe, Hartford Whalers, April 11, 1980

Toronto's King Clancy once joked, "They ought to bottle Gordie Howe's sweat. It would make a great liniment to rub on hockey players." But what would we call it, Methuselah Musk? No other individual in North American sports can rival Howe's incredible durability. The ageless wonder played *all* 80 games of the 1979–80 schedule for the NHL's Hartford Whalers at age 51 (he turned 52 just before the season's end), then skated in three playoff matches versus Montreal; his last, a 4–3 overtime loss on April 11, 1980. And Howe wasn't just taking up space on Hartford's bench. He posted 41 points that season, pushing his NHL career total to an eye-popping 1,850—and opposing players less than half his age were still keeping a respectful distance from his infamous elbows. Howe counted his last regular-season point, a goal, against Detroit's Rogie Vachon on April 6, 1980. It came an astounding 34 years after his first NHL point, a goal, scored in his first NHL game against Toronto's Turk Broda on October 16, 1946. Of course, Howe's NHL numbers don't include the 508 points he picked up in six WHA seasons, including a 102-point campaign at age 48 with the Houston Aeros. All told, Mr. Hockey's career spanned 32 pro seasons and 2,421 NHL and WHA games.

MOST SHUTOUTS BY A GOALIE IN ONE PLAYOFF YEAR

7: Martin Brodeur, New Jersey Devils, 2003

It might be pure skill, circumstance or even Lady Luck that leads to one exceptional game or season, but every NHL record-maker holds some extra advantage over the next guy. In Martin Brodeur's case, as magnificent as his play was in 2003, he was backstopping a defense-first team that choked the life out of its opponents with traps, dump-ins and dump-outs. And before obstructions were called by the book in 2005–06, no club benefited more from referee leniency and the suffocating style of hockey it wrought than New Jersey. The Devils constructed a winner and secured a legacy of three championships in eight years. The winning formula proved to be timely offense and killer defense, with the core of their system the stellar work of Brodeur. Not many goalies could take the relentless pressure of playing a defensive team game. Brodeur excelled at it, acting like a third defenseman on the ice. And in 2003, he put together a textbook display of netminding in a 16-win Cup race, netting shutouts in each series, with two against Boston, one versus Tampa Bay and Ottawa and three to push Anaheim to the brink in finals play. In any other year, his netminding would be MVP-worthy, but Jean-Sebastien Giguere stole the Conn Smythe Trophy with a monster performance for the Ducks in the first three rounds.

MOST POINTS BY A DEFENSEMAN IN ONE PLAYOFF YEAR

37: Paul Coffey, Edmonton Oilers, 1985

Calling Paul Coffey a defenseman is akin to describing one-time team-mate Mark Messier as just a forward. Coffey was a world-class skater with a complete inventory of shots, passes and plays that gave the Oilers another dimension of offensive skill: one that came from the blue line. In postseason play, Coffey owns five of the six NHL scoring records for rearguards, all produced in 1985, when he set new game and year marks in the categories of goals, assists and points. The hockey world had never seen such a display of firepower from a defenseman in one Cup run, including Coffey's best offensive game: a six-pointer on one goal and five assists against Chicago on May 14. The effort fuelled Coffey to a 37-point postseason, a stunning 12 points more than the total of previous record-holder Denis Potvin, who collected 25 points in 1981. Brian Leetch netted a close-second 34 points in 1994, but the Rangers D-man needed five more games (23) to approach Coffey's output. In the 1985 finals against Philadelphia, Coffey was methodically throwing checks, blocking shots and racking up more points. He would match Wayne Gretzky's point production in the series with three goals and eight assists, including the Stanley Cup winner, but fell just one short of the finals record of 12, owned only by forwards.

HIGHEST PLUS-MINUS IN ONE GAME

Plus-10: Tom Bladon, Philadelphia Flyers, December 11, 1977

Tom Bladon must have been doing some deep thinking about coach Fred Shero's plan to hire psychologists to boost Philadelphia's goal output, which could explain why, in 1977–78, the rearguard generated one of the greatest single-game performances in NHL history. Bladon seemingly channelled Bobby Orr that one night in December 1977, when he scored four goals and four assists for a spooky eight points. Orr's spirit worked so well on Bladon's psyche that the blueliner with the heavy shot became the first player to break one of Orr's 14 league records, topping No. 4's prestigious seven-point mark to become only the fourth NHLer ever to score eight or more points in a game. And each point came at even strength, which equals Maurice Richard's mark for the most points in a game without a power-play point. Even more impressive, Bladon concluded the Flyers' 11–1 gutting of the Cleveland Barons with a record plus-10. Bladon was on the ice for every Philadelphia marker except its fifth, while Cleveland's lone score came on the power play with 1:45 remaining and Bladon on the bench. Bladon subsequently predicted that his plus-10 would be "tougher to beat than eight points." And he was right. Paul Coffey tied his single-game point record in March 1986, but Bladon's plus-10 still stands alone.

MOST GOALS WITHOUT A POWER-PLAY GOAL IN ONE SEASON

31: *Doug Smail, Winnipeg Jets, 1984–85*

Although he played 13 NHL seasons, Doug Smail remains a largely for-
gotten player, much like this record. But it merits a second look: very
few players get close to the 30-goal mark without scoring on the power
play. Delete Tim Kerr's 34 power-play markers from his 58-goal season
in 1985–86, and he is left with 24. Yet Smail somehow found a way to
score 31 times without a sniff of work on the power play in 1984–85. That
year, the Jets' roster included an NHL-record six 30-goal men, including
the opportunistic Smail. With Dale Hawerchuk, Paul MacLean and
Brian Mullen powering the first line, Smail took up residence on the
checking unit. Despite his defensive role he became the Jets' busiest
forward, "bustling every shift, hitting the holes, creating others, driving
past, between and behind defensemen," according to the *Hockey News*.
And though Smail played with different linemates, he was consistently
the sparkplug of his unit. "We were always assigned the roles of checkers. We were never asked to think offensively. But the game is based
on who scores the most goals. I think we can help in that regard," said
Smail, who finished with a respectable plus-12. It proved to be Winnipeg's best season in franchise history, as the Jets finished with 96 points,
fourth overall in the NHL.

HIGHEST SAVE PERCENTAGE BY A GOALIE IN ONE SEASON

.937: Dominik Hasek, Buffalo Sabres, 1998–99

Dominik Hasek broke all the rules. The Czech goalkeeper dropped his stick and covered loose pucks with his blocker, stopped shots lying flat on his back, head-butted pucks with his helmet and twisted his body in crazy contortions that prompted some to suggest he had a Slinky for a spine. "They say I am unorthodox, that I flop around the ice like some kind of fish," Hasek once admitted. "I say, who cares as long as I stop the puck?" And that he did. During the 1990s, there was no better goalie on the planet. Despite tending net for a mediocre Buffalo Sabres team, the man from Pardubice won five Vezina Trophies in six years from 1994 to 1999, led the NHL in save percentage in six straight seasons, claimed Hart Trophies as MVP in 1997 and 1998 and sparked the Czech Republic to a gold medal at the 1998 Winter Olympics. Hasek was so consistently brilliant that it is difficult to single out one highlight season, but 1998–99 was a doozy. The Dominator posted nine shutouts and a stingy 1.87 goals-against average, while stopping 1,758 of 1,877 shots for a stunning save percentage of .937. The performance erased Hasek's NHL record of .932, set the season before, and established a lofty standard that will be very tough for future goalies to conquer.

HIGHEST CAREER WINNING-PERCENTAGE BY A GOALIE

.758: Ken Dryden, Montreal Canadiens, 1970–71 to 1978–79

The most enduring image of Ken Dryden is his "thinker's pose," the posture he assumed when the action left his zone. With the tip of his goalie stick dug into the ice and his arms folded across the knob, he resembled a masked chess player plotting his next move. But winning, not thinking, was Dryden's true calling card. After being promoted from the minors late in 1970–71, the long-limbed rookie won all six of his starts in impressive fashion. And Montreal stuck with the youngster in the playoffs, where his stellar netminding sparked the Habs to the Stanley Cup and earned him the Conn Smythe Trophy as playoff MVP. No other player with so little NHL experience has ever won the award. Still, though Dryden was fortunate to join a team that was evolving into a powerhouse, being the starting goalie for Montreal posed a unique challenge. The team was expected not just to succeed, but to win Stanley Cups. As Dryden noted, "Most envy me my job, some are not so sure." Dryden retired with a record of 258 wins, 57 losses and 74 ties. His career .758-winning-percentage is easily the best among goalies with 200 wins or more. Predictably, he also owns the NHL record for highest career winning-percentage in the playoffs, a mark of .714.

LONGEST CONSECUTIVE-GAMES GOAL-SCORING
STREAK IN ONE PLAYOFF YEAR

10 games: Reggie Leach, Philadelphia Flyers, April 17 to May 9, 1976

They called him "the Rifle," and it was the perfect nickname, given that Reggie Leach had several devastating shots in his repertoire: a wicked 100 m.p.h. slap shot, a hard, accurate wrist shot and a tricky backhander. He would also shoot often and from almost any angle, and, because his release was so quick, he often caught goaltenders off balance. Leach's scoring skills were showcased in 1975–76, when he netted a league-leading 61 goals playing on Philadelphia's LCB Line with Bobby Clarke and Bill Barber. The right-winger then continued to torment opposition goalies in the playoffs, scoring in a record 10 straight games. But his most dazzling performance came in the Flyers' series-clinching 6–3 win against Boston in Game 5 of the semifinals, when he notched five goals—three of them on backhanders—that completely bamboozled Bruins goalie Gilles Gilbert. The five goals tied the NHL record for most playoff tallies in a game, but the Rifle still had some bullets left. He potted four of the Flyers' nine goals to lead all scorers in the finals and set a new postseason mark of 19. The results were bittersweet for Leach, who copped the playoff MVP trophy while his team was swept by Montreal in the finals.

MOST CONSECUTIVE IMPROVED SEASONS BY A COACH

6: Al Arbour, New York Islanders, 1973–74 to 1978–79

Al Arbour captured Stanley Cups with three different NHL clubs as a defenseman—for Detroit, Chicago and Toronto—before winning another four Cups as the coach of the New York Islanders. His achievement of improving the Isles' point totals in six consecutive seasons, while less familiar than his playoff exploits, remains unequalled in coaching annals. After almost doubling team points to 56 in his first season on Long Island in 1973–74, Arbour steered his club to records of 88, 101, 106, 111 and 116 by developing a system that taught his players defense. Coupled with fresh talent in star players such as Mike Bossy and Denis Potvin, Arbour turned the Islanders from playoff pretenders into contenders, then into postseason favourites during the next five seasons. The steady rise ended in 1979–80, with a slump to 91 points, when, after several playoff setbacks, Arbour decided to place less emphasis on regular-season finishes and instead focus on postseason performance. The acquisition of Butch Goring in March 1980 provided the Islanders' last missing component. Two months later, Arbour's club went on to win its first of four consecutive Cups.

69

HIGHEST GOALS-PER-GAME AVERAGE IN ONE PLAYOFF YEAR

1.70: Edouard "Newsy" Lalonde, Montreal Canadiens, 1919

If the measure of a record's greatness is its longevity, then Newsy Lalonde's playoff scoring feats rank among the best—they went unchallenged for more than a half-century. During 10 postseason games in 1919, Lalonde notched 17 goals (11 of them in the NHL finals against Ottawa), a total that endured until Reggie Leach and Jari Kurri scored 19 times in their longer playoff schedules of 1976 and 1985. Lalonde was early hockey's most colourful player. He won scoring titles in four different pro leagues and was Montreal's captain, playing coach and original Flying Frenchman. A born leader and a great fighter, his fierce temper was unleashed on opponents, spectators—even teammates—come game time. In 1919, after battering Ottawa, Lalonde's Canadiens faced the west coast champion Seattle Metropolitans in the Cup finals. The all-purpose Lalonde switched between centre and defense and, to master western rules, even played rover (old-time hockey's free-wheeling seventh-man position). In Game 2, reports said "it was practically Lalonde against Seattle... when he scored all the Canadiens' goals" in the 4–2 win. Sadly, the playoffs were suspended without the Cup being awarded after several players were hospitalized with influenza. Lalonde's amazing run was over, only adding to his notoriety and fame.

HIGHEST PERCENTAGE OF A TEAM'S GOALS
IN ONE SEASON (MODERN-DAY)

29.5: Pavel Bure, Florida Panthers, 2000–01

With his breakaway speed, shifty moves and lethal shot, Pavel Bure was the go-to guy on every team he played for. But in 2000–01, with Florida, Bure was literally the only guy. The toothless Panthers had absolutely no supporting cast. Yet, that year, the Russian Rocket led the league in goal scoring for the second straight season, twinkling the twine 59 times and accounting for a modern-day NHL-record 29.5 per cent of Florida's 200 total goals. (Viktor Kozlov placed a distant second with 14.) It's scary to imagine where Florida might have ended up if not for Bure, who either scored or assisted on 46 per cent of the club's goals. The blue-eyed Muscovite's one-man show in the Sunshine State didn't carry Florida into the playoffs, but it did break Brett Hull's mark of 27.7 per cent, set in 1990–91, when Hull scored 86 of the Blues' 310 goals. And though Bure's standard lags far behind Joe Malone's all-time record of 42.9 per cent, set in 1919–20, when Malone bagged 39 of the Quebec Bulldogs' 91 goals, it's impossible to draw a fair comparison between the two eras. In Malone's day, the rosters were tiny and some skaters remained on the ice for the entire game, while Bure had to share his playing time with 17 other players.

HIGHEST WINNING PERCENTAGE BY A TEAM IN ONE SEASON

.875: Boston Bruins, 1929–30

The Bruins ruled with an iron claw in 1929–30, compiling a 38–5–1 record while leading the league in goals scored and fewest goals allowed. Their imposing attack was led by the Dynamite Line of Cooney Weiland, Dit Clapper and Dutch Gainor, who combined to tally 102 goals in the 44-game schedule. Hall of Famers Eddie Shore and Lionel Hitchman anchored a rock-solid defense and ace goalie Tiny Thompson won the Vezina Trophy with a 2.19 goals-against average. Only one team, the Montreal Maroons, beat the Bruins at Boston Garden in 1929–30, and that was an early season contest that Shore missed due to injuries sustained in a series of violent altercations with the Maroons in Boston's previous game. After that loss, the Bruins reeled off 20 straight victories on home ice. The next year they lost only once at the Garden, which gave them a towering 37–2–5 home record over the two seasons. But the Bruins' dominance did not carry over into the 1930 playoffs. After edging the Maroons in a rugged best-of-five semifinals, they were upset two games to none by the Montreal Canadiens in the best-of-three finals. Those two losses not only cost Boston the Stanley Cup, but also its status as the NHL's greatest team of all time.

MOST CONSECUTIVE UNANSWERED GOALS

25: New York Rangers, February 3 to 11, 1973

Although often overshadowed by the explosive Boston Bruins, the New York Rangers teams of the early 1970s were legitimate offensive dynamos. The club's attack was spearheaded by the line of Jean Ratelle, Rod Gilbert and Vic Hadfield, nicknamed the GAG Line—short for Goal-A-Game. But in truth, the line was more effective than the name implies: in 1971–72, the trio scored 139 goals in 78 games. However, it was during the 1972–73 season that the Blueshirts set this little-known record, pumping in 25 goals without a response from their opponents during a five-game span in February. The streak began when the Rangers counted the final five goals in a 7–3 whipping of the Bruins. A scheduling quirk that saw them play three straight games against the NHL's two expansion teams, the Atlanta Flames and New York Islanders, helped propel the Rangers to the record, with three consecutive 6–0 shutouts. New York then notched the first two goals in its next game versus Montreal before Frank Mahovlich snapped the spell, beating goalie Ed Giacomin 54 seconds into the third period of a 2–2 tie. The only team to approach New York's record is the Philadelphia Flyers, who scored 23 unanswered goals in a four-game span, October 15 to 22, 1977.

MOST POINTS BY A ROOKIE DEFENSEMAN IN ONE SEASON

76: Larry Murphy, Los Angeles Kings, 1980–81

When Larry Murphy broke into the NHL, many observers felt he played more like a forward who occasionally skated backwards to protect his net. He was more positional than physical; a finesse player working in the demanding role of crease-clearer and shot-blocker. The offensive risks he took by pinching in or playing the puck instead of the body were overlooked because his natural skating and puckhandling skills generated such big offense. He could go end-to-end, make a breakaway pass and deliver a deft backhand shot or forehand slapper. Yet, for all this, Murphy was rarely as conspicuous during his lengthy career as he was with Los Angeles as a 19-year-old in 1980–81. The youth-oriented Kings certainly made his transition from junior hockey to the NHL memorable. He finished fourth in team scoring, just behind the Triple Crown Line of Marcel Dionne, Dave Taylor and Charlie Simmer, each of whom finished in the NHL's top 10. His startling 76-point effort broke the freshman mark of 65 (set the year before by Ray Bourque), and his 60 assists earned him another all-time record. Yet Murphy initially doubted he could make the Kings. He claimed to have no trouble playing; it was the thinking part of the game that gave him concern, because everything moved so fast. Not too fast, apparently.

74

MOST GAME-WINNING GOALS IN ONE PLAYOFF YEAR

7: Brad Richards, Tampa Bay Lightning, 2004

Every Stanley Cup championship team ices one—a playoff hero who elevates his team to victory with spectacular play. Brad Richards was that player for Tampa Bay in 2004. You could build a case for Nikolai Khabibulin, the all-world goalie with a 1.71 goals-against average, or Dave Andreychuk, the Bolts' inspirational captain, who did as much to win the Cup in the dressing room as on the ice. But Richards was named playoff MVP for a reason. The 24-year-old centre scored 12 goals and added 14 assists for a playoff-high 26 points to capture the Conn Smythe and the imaginations of hockey fans everywhere, including those in his hometown of Murray Harbour, P.E.I. Of course, his big reward was Stanley, a prize no one expected the Lightning to win. To do it, Richards played clutch hockey, scoring a record seven game-winners in almost half of the Lightning's playoff victories, with each one altering the game's momentum—and often the flow of a series. To keep his team positioned to win, Richards delivered several timely goals, key tie-breakers and one decisive marker in overtime; Tampa Bay was 9–0 when he scored a goal. But his heroics were greatest during the finals against Calgary, when he had four goals and nine points. Richards's seven winners broke the mark of six held by Joe Sakic and Joe Nieuwendyk.

MOST PENALTY MINUTES BY A SCORING CHAMPION

154: Stan Mikita, Chicago Blackhawks, 1964–65

Stan Mikita's mid-career conversion from Mr. Nasty to Mr. Clean is one of the most radical personality changes witnessed in an NHL player. Though only five foot eight and 155 pounds when he entered the league, Mikita was a chippy, abrasive character. In Montreal they dubbed him "le Petit Diable," the Little Devil. And with "Terrible" Ted Lindsay as his linemate and mentor in his rookie season, Mikita perfected his hatchet-work. In 1963–64, he won his first scoring title with 89 points—while logging 146 penalty minutes, the most of any NHL scoring champion. Then in 1964–65, Mikita claimed another scoring crown with 154 PIM, breaking his own record. Incredibly, only two years later, the Chicago centre won the Art Ross Trophy with 97 points—but this time with just 12 PIM, which is still the record for fewest penalty minutes by a scoring champion in a minimum 70-game schedule. Mikita also won the Lady Byng Trophy as the league's most gentlemanly player and the Hart Trophy as MVP. It was a triple feat he repeated the next year. The change in playing style came about because Mikita realized he was more valuable to his team on the ice than cooling his heels in the sin bin. As he admitted, "You need a hell of a long stick to score from the penalty box."

MOST CAREER POINTS IN THE PLAYOFF FINALS

62: Jean Béliveau, Montreal Canadiens, 1953–54 to 1970–71

The incredible 12 Stanley Cup finals that Jean Béliveau participated in are probably the main reasons the legendary Montreal Canadiens captain owns such an important record. Still, he had to get to the big dance and perform big in each series—under intense pressure and scrutiny—as Montreal's team leader, in a potboiler city where championships were once a rite of spring. Clearly, with enough Stanley Cup rings for each finger, Béliveau was no perimeter player, particularly in finals action. In 64 games, he scored 30 goals and 32 assists for a record 62 points—only Maurice Richard has more goals and Wayne Gretzky more assists in the finals. But it's Béliveau's career power-play numbers that reveal the real story of his success. The Canadiens counted on Le Gros Bill in almost every man-advantage situation in 12 of 13 final rounds, except for the 1959 series when he cracked two vertebrae in the semifinals. He also scored an NHL-high 27 career points on the power play and established still-standing marks for power-play goals (11) and power-play assists (16), and remained dominant throughout his lengthy career. In his first finals of 1956, he produced a modern-day record of seven goals. Fifteen years later, in his final victory lap, the 40-year-old captain bagged four points against Chicago.

MOST POINTS IN ONE PLAYOFF GAME

8: *Patrik Sundstrom, New Jersey Devils, April 22, 1988*
8: *Mario Lemieux, Pittsburgh Penguins, April 25, 1989*

It all began harmlessly enough for Patrik Sundstrom. Just 10 minutes into the third game of the New Jersey–Washington divisional finals, the Devils centre earned an assist on a goal by Ken Daneyko. The scoring continued at a record pace, as assists and goals piled up, and, before long, Sundstrom had equalled Wayne Gretzky's playoff mark of seven points. The 26-year-old Swede knew he had big points on the night, but he didn't realize Gretzky held the record or that he had tied it until officials at Brendan Byrne Arena made the announcement. "It was kind of strange out there for a while," said Sundstrom in disbelief that he was being mentioned in the same breath as the Great One. Then, with just 5:46 remaining in the game, he skated into the Capitals' zone and lifted a soft backhand past goalie Clint Malarchuk. The goal, his third of the night, gave Sundstrom eight points and a new league record in the 10–4 triumph. The following year, Mario Lemieux recorded five goals and three assists in a 10–7 win against Philadelphia—a brilliant offensive show, and Lemieux's third eight-point game since the previous October. For Sundstrom, sharing the mark with Lemieux just made his record all the more special.

MOST GOALS BY A PENALTY-MINUTE LEADER IN ONE SEASON

35: Tiger Williams, Vancouver Canucks, 1980–81

Pugilists aren't hired to be goal scorers. If they bury a few while leading the charge, it's a bonus. In Tiger Williams, the NHL's all-time most-penalized player, what his coaches got was one of the premier tough guys of the 1970s and 1980s, one who had no illusions about his first priority on the ice. But his coaches also knew Williams had a nose for the net. Though his rap sheet of assault charges, multiple-game suspensions and misconducts for stick-swinging, biting and head-butting characterizes his 962-game career, Williams also forged a minor reputation for his offensive play, and particularly for his wild ride-on-his stick celebration skates after scoring. It was a trick he claims to have done only once, even though he dented the twine 241 times. Sure, he averaged four minutes of penalties every game, but in every fourth game Williams counted a goal—a startling average that proves he was a decent scorer. Some of hockey's most productive forwards don't own that kind of career percentage. Nor can many players claim a 35-goal season such as Williams had with the Canucks in 1980–81, when he amassed a league-high 343 penalty minutes. During his 14-year NHL rampage, Williams had a lot of opponents in his crosshairs, including goalies.

MOST SHOTS FACED BY A WINNING GOALIE
IN A REGULAR-SEASON GAME

68: Mario Lessard, Los Angeles Kings, March 24, 1981
68: Jake Forbes, New York Americans, December 26, 1925

Although both the NHL record books and newspaper accounts credit Jake Forbes with stopping 67 of 68 shots in a 3–1 win over the Pittsburgh Pirates in 1925, one has to doubt the accuracy of the number. Pirates goalie Roy Worters reportedly blocked 70 of 73 shots in the same game, which means the two teams combined for an unbelievable 141 shots on goal—in an era when forward passing was forbidden. In contrast, Mario Lessard's stunning performance in 1981 is the genuine article. Lessard virtually beat Minnesota single-handedly, stopping 65 of 68 shots as Los Angeles beat the North Stars 4–3. Although badly outplayed for most of the game, the Kings netted four goals in an eight-and-a-half-minute span in the second period to take a 4–2 lead into the intermission. In the third, the North Stars blasted 26 shots on net without a reply, ending with a 29–2 edge for the period, but only Steve Christoff managed to beat the Kings' beleaguered goalkeeper. The final shot totals were ridiculously one-sided: Minnesota, 68; Los Angeles, 19. Lessard finished the season with a league-leading 35 wins, but the most difficult was the one he recorded in Bloomington on March 24, 1981.

FASTEST HAT TRICK BY A PLAYER ON ONE POWER PLAY

44 seconds: Jean Béliveau, Montreal Canadiens, November 5, 1955

Jean Béliveau notched 18 hat tricks in his NHL career, but the most significant was the one he posted on November 5, 1955. Since the creation of the NHL in 1917, penalized players always had to serve the full duration of their infractions, even if their opponents scored. No one had ever objected to the rule, but in 1955–56, as Montreal's power-play unit of Béliveau, Maurice Richard, Bert Olmstead, Doug Harvey and Bernie Geoffrion began scoring multiple times on the same man-advantage, other teams began to squawk. And after Béliveau's outburst in November versus Boston, the grousing grew louder. The Bruins were up 2–0 in the second period when they made the fatal error of taking two minor penalties. During the subsequent two-man advantage, Béliveau put three pucks past goalie Terry Sawchuk in 44 seconds. He later added a fourth goal to seal a 4–2 victory. Aided by its lethal power play, Montreal went on to win 45 games (outpacing second-place Detroit by 24 points), then capped the year by taking the Stanley Cup. After the season, the NHL Board of Governors proposed a rule change that would enable a player serving a minor penalty to return to the ice if the opposition scored. The rule carried by a 5–1 margin, with Montreal casting the lone dissenting vote.

AGE OF YOUNGEST AND OLDEST PLAYOFF SCORING LEADER

21 years, one month; and 36 years, one month:
Gordie Howe, Detroit Red Wings, 1949 and 1964

It's not hard to believe that Gordie Howe is the only NHLer in history to own both the youngest and oldest player records in an important statistical category. In 1949, Howe's third postseason, Detroit played a gruelling seven-game semifinal series against Montreal. The Production Line of Howe, Ted Lindsay and Sid Abel scored 12 of the Red Wings' 17 goals, eight of them off Howe's stick. But in the finals, Toronto surprised the weary Wings in a four-game sweep. Still, Howe, 21 years old, collected 11 points and his first scoring title in playoff action. During the next six years, Detroit would turn into a powerhouse, winning four Stanley Cups. Meanwhile, Howe established himself as a clutch playoff performer, earning another five scoring titles—his sixth and final coming 15 years later in 1964, again against a two-time defending Cup champion Toronto team in the finals. (Howe scored four times against the Maple Leafs, but Detroit fell in Game 7 of the series.) At age 36, Howe led all postseason scorers, with nine goals and 19 points. Howe never had a best-before date. He went on to outlast and outplay all of his contemporaries, notching his final NHL goal on April 9, 1980, at age 52.

MOST CONSECUTIVE GAMES
ALLOWING TWO GOALS OR LESS (MODERN-DAY)

18: Jacques Plante, Montreal Canadiens,
October 22 to December 2, 1959

On almost any other team, Jacques Plante would have been the best player, but on the Montreal Canadiens' dynasty squads of the 1950s, where superstars filled almost every position, Plante was merely as great as everyone else. This one-two punch between Montreal's ferocious scoring power and Plante's brilliance in the crease brought the Canadiens their most enduring legacy: five consecutive Stanley Cups. And in 1959–60, Montreal proved just how superbly balanced its offense and defense was when, within a game of each other in a six-week period, two daunting records were set. During the Canadiens' unprecedented tear of scoring the first goal in 18 straight games, between October 18 and November 29, Plante produced the NHL's longest modern-era streak of games allowing two goals or less. (George Hainsworth and Roy Worters had longer streaks in the 1920s.) But both Montreal records will forever be overshadowed by Plante's decision to wear a mask during the seventh game of the streak. Ironically, at the time, the revolutionary move was viewed as just another eccentric gesture by a neurotic netminder.

MOST PENALTY MINUTES IN ONE SEASON

472: Dave Schultz, Philadelphia Flyers, 1974–75

They come and they go, but no one has yet knocked out the Hammer as the NHL's leading goon brawler. In 1974–75, his greatest season of savagery, Dave Schultz carved out a record 472 minutes—the equivalent of almost eight complete games—cooling in the box. Surprisingly, Schultz once scored 20 goals in a season. But he chose to play the heavy. "I'd rather fight than score. Scoring is over in a second, but a good fight can last awhile, and you've got time to enjoy it," he once said. These days, tough guys need real hockey skills to make it in the NHL and, once there, have to contend with the instigator rule, which makes Schultz's hitman mark look as far out of reach for today's players as Wayne Gretzky's 92-goal season. But in the '70s, Schultz was the backbone of the Flyers' Broad Street Bullies identity. During his prime, from 1972–73 to 1975–76, Schultz sat out 1,386 minutes and accounted for almost 20 per cent of all box time amassed by Philadelphia, the NHL's most penalized and destructive team. And after the Flyers won two Stanley Cups, many clubs attempted to copy their approach to the game. As for Schultz, he changed the record books and likely the rule book, which introduced the instigator penalty in 1976–77.

AGE OF YOUNGEST PLAYER TO SCORE A HAT TRICK

18 years, 153 days: Jordan Staal,
Pittsburgh Penguins, February 10, 2007

Scary. That's the best way to describe Jordan Staal's rookie season. No, Staal didn't dethrone Teemu Selanne as top rookie goal scorer, but then Selanne wasn't a teenager playing in his draft year with a league average of less than six goals per game. What made Staal scary good during his 29-goal freshman campaign was the number of "youngest" records he chiselled in stone—on the penalty kill and on penalty shots. With seven shorthanded goals setting a new league mark, at even strength Staal was a giant on Pittsburgh's second line. On his best rookie night, he scored three times on Toronto's Andrew Raycroft to end former Maple Leafs forward Jack Hamilton's 64-year reign as the youngest NHL hat-trickster. Hamilton was 18 years and 185 days old when he scored four goals on December 4, 1943. Stall, a month younger than Hamilton, netted the game's first two goals in five-on-five situations, then, in overtime, notched a breathtaking winner that belied his experience or years. After a pinpoint pass from Evgeni Malkin, Staal cut sharp to his left and patiently waited for Toronto defenseman Bryan McCabe to slide by. He then whipped a low shot beyond Raycroft to complete the hat trick. It was a night of hockey that had everyone shaking their heads in disbelief.

AVERAGE AGE OF OLDEST STANLEY CUP-WINNING TEAM

31 years: Toronto Maple Leafs, 1967

Few hockey fans gave the Leafs a realistic shot at winning the Cup in 1966–67. In decline since its last Cup triumph in 1964, the club had little scoring prowess and a roster filled with creaky veterans. Seven Leafs were aged 36 or older: Johnny Bower (42), Allan Stanley (41), Red Kelly (39), Terry Sawchuk (37), Tim Horton (37), Marcel Pronovost (36) and George Armstrong (36). And all that experience did not help during the regular season, as Toronto limped home in third place, 19 points behind first-place Chicago—but it paid dividends in the playoffs. Playing cagey, opportunistic hockey, the Leafs upset the high-flying Blackhawks in the first round, then continued to confound the critics in the finals as their liniment-soaked lineup thwarted the younger and faster Montreal Canadiens. Before Game 6, with Toronto leading the series three games to two, coach Punch Imlach then addressed his troops: "Some of you have been with me for nine years. It's been said that I stuck with the old ones so long we couldn't possibly win the Stanley Cup. For some of you, it's a farewell. Go out there and ram the puck down their goddamn throats." The old warhorses fulfilled Imlach's request, beating their archrivals 3–1 to claim the Cup and bring down the curtain on the Original Six era.

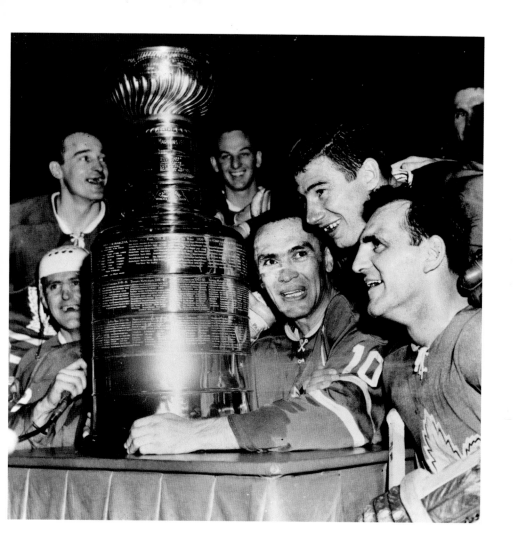

MOST CONSECUTIVE GOALS IN ONE GAME

15: Detroit Red Wings, January 23, 1944

The New York Rangers were truly pathetic in 1943–44. With a roster ravaged by World War II recruiting, the club staggered to a 6–39–5 record. Things were so desperate in Manhattan that 42-year-old coach Frank Boucher, who had been retired for five years, returned to the ice. The Rangers' main tormentor was Detroit, who outscored New York 67–26 in their 10 meetings that season. But the worst thrashing took place on January 23, when the Wings stomped the Blueshirts 15–0, the most one-sided shutout in NHL history. Rookie goalkeeper Connie Dion posted the goose egg, the only one in his 38-game career. It may have been Dion's easiest game—the shots were 58 to 9 in Detroit's favour. Rangers netminder Ken "Tubby" McAuley, a 22-year-old from the Saskatchewan senior leagues, was the victim of the shelling. If the game had lasted another second, Detroit would have scored 16 goals, as a shot went into the Rangers' net at the final buzzer. Amazingly, the Wings notched their last five goals after the 14:00-minute mark of the third period, and Syd Howe bagged a hat trick in the last six minutes. The score at this point was 10–0. Talk about humiliating a helpless opponent. The devastated Rangers did not win another game the entire season.

FEWEST GAMES NEEDED TO RECORD 300 WINS BY A COACH

525: Toe Blake, Montreal Canadiens,
October 6, 1955, to January 3, 1963

It is very difficult to coach a great team and keep it psyched. And with few exceptions, including Glen Sather, who finished just three games shy of this mark with 528, rookie coaches have seldom been blessed with more elite players than Toe Blake. During his record march to 300 wins, Blake could send out any one of three scoring champions and many more trophy-winners or All-Stars. On his 1956 Stanley Cup squad, Blake had 10 future Hall of Famers—or about half his bench. Even Montreal's rank-and-file were good enough to be first-liners on most other clubs. But for all their skill, what kept the Canadiens successful for so long was Blake's obstinate, single-minded desire to win. He came by it honestly. The great taskmaster was a very hard loser. Still, he had a tremendous feel for his team and, perhaps most important, he kept the volatile Maurice Richard in line. Blake's perfectionism, both in game preparation and during the match, pushed everyone to the limit. To maintain the edge in a dressing room of extroverts and egomaniacs, he ruled with an iron hand, knowing what a glorious team was assembled under him and the expectations of hockey-mad Montreal. It was said that Blake faced more pressure as a winning coach than most coaches do as losers.

MOST SHOTS ON GOAL BY A ROOKIE IN ONE SEASON

425: Alexander Ovechkin, Washington Capitals, 2005–06

How is it that a rookie could register the fourth-highest shot count in NHL history? Granted, that history only dates to 1967, when stats were first tabulated, but it's still almost unimaginable that a first-year player could clock the ice time to ring up totals that top most of those registered by hockey's leading triggermen. For starters, the rookie is Alexander Ovechkin, a once-in-a-generation player despite the fact that he entered the league with Sidney Crosby. Blessed with a hair-trigger release and a deceptive and deadly accurate shot, Ovechkin can score from any position on the ice. Just ask goalie Brian Boucher, who got beat in January 2006 when the Russian rookie potted the season's prettiest goal—tapping the puck blindly into the net while sliding on his back towards the corner boards. Secondly, Ovechkin played on the talent-starved Washington Capitals. In rebuilding mode, the Caps gave their number one pick 21:35 minutes of ice per game under nearly obstruction-free rules. Ovechkin's 425 shots topped Teemu Selanne's rookie mark of 387 in 1992–93 and every other player's total in 2005–06. It was an NHL first by a rookie. The Russian winger was so consistent that he scored against 22 of the Capitals' opponents, the most teams any rookie has scored upon in league history.

LONGEST PLAYOFF GAME

176 minutes, 30 seconds:
Montreal Maroons vs. Detroit Red Wings, March 24 to 25, 1936

The 9,000 fans gathered at the Montreal Forum to watch the Montreal Maroons host the Detroit Red Wings in the opening game of the 1936 playoffs had no inkling of how long a night it would be. The teams battled through 60 scoreless minutes of regulation and nearly two hours of overtime before a winner was decided. Yet despite its fabled place in history, the contest was no great spectacle. Newspaper accounts describe it as a cautious, tight-checking struggle. We can only imagine how slow the pace must have been. After a few periods of overtime, players would have been in a state of exhaustion, their gloves, uniforms and equipment soaking wet. And without ice-grooming machines, the ice would have been snowy and choppy—impossible conditions for crisp passing and skating. The slow-motion marathon ended in the sixth overtime when Detroit's Modere "Mud" Bruneteau, a rookie who had scored only two goals during the season, was given a rare shift, in which he slipped around the Maroons' defense, took a pass and beat goalie Lorne Chabot. "It was the funniest thing," Bruneteau recalled of his famous goal. "The puck just stuck there in the twine and didn't fall to the ice." Hockey's longest game was over at 2:25 a.m., and Bruneteau's legend was assured.

LONGEST WINNING STREAK BY A GOALIE

17 games: Gilles Gilbert, Boston Bruins,
December 26, 1975, to March 5, 1976

During his seven years in Boston, Gilles Gilbert posted a 155–53–41 record—good enough for an impressive .705 winning percentage, but not good enough to win the hearts of Bruins fans or the confidence of coach Don Cherry. Gilbert's unforgivable sin was his failure to lead the Bruins to a Stanley Cup, though they got close several times. In 1975–76, the slim, stringy-haired goalie from St-Espirit, Quebec, won 33 games and compiled a record 17-game winning streak that was doubly surprising, as it occurred when Bobby Orr was sidelined with a knee injury. Gilbert did have some luck along the way, though. He started but did not finish a 7–5 loss to St. Louis, with the defeat credited to his replacement, Dave Reece. And Gilbert was out with an injury on the night Toronto's Darryl Sittler went crazy and scored 10 points in an 11–4 rout of the Bruins. His streak finally ended with a 4–3 loss to the lowly California Seals. A few weeks later, Boston was knocked out of the playoffs by Philadelphia, by which time Gilbert was sharing netminding duties with Gerry Cheevers, who had just rejoined the Bruins after three years in the WHA. The next season, Cherry relegated Gilbert to backup and made Cheevers his number one puck stopper.

MOST GOALS BY A ROOKIE DEFENSEMAN IN ONE SEASON

23: Brian Leetch, New York Rangers, 1988–89

Everything went right for Brian Leetch in 1988–89. In his first full NHL season, the 20-year-old scored 71 points, the second-highest point count ever by a freshman rearguard, and bested Barry Beck's 22-goal tear of 1977–78 with a new record of 23 for rookie defensemen. Under Rangers coach Michel Bergeron's explosive, breakneck attack, Leetch thrived and quickly demonstrated his electrifying raw talent, turning his first year into a Power Point presentation for puck-carrying defensemen. Bergeron had Leetch on the ice in any situation for upwards of 25 minutes per night. The puck rarely seemed to leave his stick. He controlled the point and ran the power play. Almost half of his goals came on special teams, with eight registered on the man-advantage and three shorthanded. His hard, accurate shot and superior defensive skills made him a game-breaking defenseman, one who was just a notch below the calibre of Bobby Orr. His confidence and poise and creative genius—in both zones—earned him the Calder Trophy as top rookie. But perhaps most important, Leetch had that sixth sense of knowing where the players and the puck were all going. By the time he gathered his Calder, the youngster was already being anointed the best defenseman to come into the league since Ray Bourque.

MOST GOALS BY A ROOKIE IN ONE PLAYOFF YEAR

14: Dino Ciccarelli, Minnesota North Stars, 1981

Hockey coaches love Cinderella stories, particularly those involving either a rookie or the playoffs. And in Dino Ciccarelli's case, Minnesota coach Glen Sonmor got both during the 1981 postseason, when Ciccarelli scripted one of the most inspiring starts to an NHL career. After badly breaking his leg during his third junior season with the London Knights, the hard-nosed gunner was passed over by every team at the NHL draft. He had scored a whack of goals for the Knights, including 72 in 68 games in 1977–78, but the knock against Ciccarelli was his five-foot-eight, 165-pound fireplug frame and the 18-inch steel rod in his leg. Then, Minnesota signed him as a free agent, and, somehow, Ciccarelli's underdog status meshed perfectly with the below-the-radar North Stars, where he was a nuisance around the net, providing stellar offense and a win-at-all-costs attitude. Led by Bobby Smith, Steve Payne and a host of playoff neophytes, including Neal Broten and Brad Palmer, Minnesota charged through three rounds before succumbing to the powerhouse New York Islanders in the finals. In 19 playoff games, Ciccarelli netted 14 goals and 21 points to smash two rookie scoring marks. Among the 22 records set that postseason, only a few remain, but they include those established by Ciccarelli during that wonderful Cup run of 1981.

MOST OVERTIME GOALS IN ONE PLAYOFF SERIES

3: *Mel Hill, Boston Bruins, 1939*

Mel Hill may be better remembered for having one of hockey's most distinctive nicknames, "Sudden Death," than the actual feat that inspired the name. A solid but unspectacular player, Hill scored a modest 10 goals for Boston in the 1938–39 season, but he emerged from the shadows to steal the spotlight in the semifinals against the New York Rangers. In Game 1, he ended a three-overtime endurance test by beating goalie Davey Kerr to secure a 2–1 Boston win. In Game 2, the right-winger came up big again, notching the sudden-death winner in a 3–2 Boston victory. After the Bruins took the next game 4–1, the Rangers rallied to win three straight, knotting the series and setting the stage for another dose of dramatics from Hill. Deadlocked 1–1 after 60 minutes, the two teams battled into a third overtime until Hill took a pass from Bill Cowley and flipped the puck past goalie Bert Gardiner. The goal gave Beantown the series and Hill a record that still stands after nearly 70 years. He became an instant celebrity, though his new nickname proved a burden. As he admitted in an interview, "It seemed like I was expected to be the hero in every playoff game from that moment on. The name "Sudden Death" was easier to live with after I retired."

MOST SHOTS FACED BY A GOALIE
IN ONE SEASON (SINCE 1954-55)

2,475: Roberto Luongo, Florida Panthers, 2003–04

Roberto Luongo has seen so much vulcanized rubber speeding in his direction, he could sponsor the entire stretch of the Trans-Canada Highway. He waited a league-record 417 games to get a taste of postseason action, and when he did, the Vancouver goalie got a mouthful, facing a modern-day NHL-high of 76 shots in a game that dragged on though seven gruelling periods. The marathon against Dallas—on April 11, 2007—was the sixth-longest match in league history. But it was no baptism by fire for the playoff rookie. If any season prepared him for such career-defining moments, it was 2003–04, when Luongo endured the greatest hail of pucks in history while backstopping the pathetic Florida Panthers. He was a warrior through 72 games, battling 2,475 shots to establish a new NHL-record and break Felix Potvin's mark of 2,438, set in 1996–97. Luongo also established a new league record with 2,303 saves, allowing only 172 goals for a .931 save percentage, the third-best in the league. Overall, he logged seven shutouts for the 24th-place Panthers. But his most impressive work may have come in three 50-shot games. Luongo won two of them and was 7–7–5 when facing 40 or more shots. It's hard to imagine how bad Florida would have been without him.

MOST PLAYOFF YEARS IN A CAREER

22: Chris Chelios, 1984 to 2007

When Hollywood was casting for Frank Miller's 300, the gore-and-sandals movie about 300 Spartans who fought a suicidal battle defending Greece against Persian invaders, filmmakers should have considered Chris Chelios. The warhorse defenseman and three-time Norris Trophy winner could have played King Leonidas of Sparta, who famously said "Come take them!" in reply to the enemy's request to lay down his army's weapons. Chelios knows the role better than most. His Spartan bloodlines don't allow for the word quit. By the time he set the league record for most playoff seasons in 2007, Chelios, at age 45, was clashing with 20- and 30-year-olds. He would become the oldest defenseman in playoff history and the second-oldest postseason performer of all time after Gordie Howe, and despite less ice time, he didn't miss a shift or lighten up on his hitting. But more than just superior genetics or his extraordinary competitiveness, which borders on nasty, it's Chelios's hardcore fitness regimen that he credits for his staying power. He trains on mountain bikes and with surfing buddies in a sprint workout called stand-up paddling. And several times a week he takes a torturous ride on a stationary bike in a sauna. To date, Chelios has made the playoffs every year except 1998 with Chicago.

MOST 30-OR-MORE-GOAL SEASONS

17: Mike Gartner, 1979–80 to 1997–98

Maybe Mike Gartner had a secret cloaking device. He was rarely in the limelight during his stellar career. Despite amassing the NHL's sixth-highest goal count of 708, there is no Art Ross Trophy on his mantle to celebrate his considerable scoring skills, no Hart Trophy for his invaluable play on five NHL teams and not a single nomination to the First or Second All-Star teams for his breakaway speed—the fastest in the league. Plus, he never won a Stanley Cup. Instead, after 19 seasons, Gartner entered retirement with only a stash of oddball records, such as being the first NHLer to reach milestones of 500 goals, 500 assists, 1,000 points and 1,000 games in the same season and owning the fastest speed-skating time (until 2003)—after turning a lap in 13.386 seconds at 1986's All-Star game skills competition. His most recognized accomplishment was his consistency over a very long period of time. Gartner netted 30 or more goals in his first 15 NHL seasons. If not for the lockout-shortened 1994–95 campaign, he would have hit the mark in 18 straight years (since two more 30-goal years followed the lockout). Gartner's cloak of anonymity finally lifted in 2001, when he was voted into the Hockey Hall of Fame in his first year of eligibility.

MOST CONSECUTIVE PLAYOFF-SERIES
WINS AGAINST ONE OPPONENT

18: Montreal Canadiens vs. Boston Bruins, 1946 to 1987

The Canadiens and Bruins have been bitter rivals since 1924, when Boston became the first American team to join the NHL and hosted Montreal in its opening game. And though both clubs have had their triumphant moments during the regular season, in the playoffs the story has been very different. During an incredible 41-year span from 1946 to 1987, for example, Montreal beat Boston like a rented mule. In that time the two teams met 18 times in the postseason and Boston failed to win a single series. The streak began when the Dick Irvin-coached Habs dumped the Dit Clapper-coached Bruins in the 1946 finals and continued through until 1988, when the Terry O'Reilly-coached Bruins mercifully snapped the jinx by beating the Jean Perron-coached Canadiens in the division finals. The 1950s was an especially cruel decade for the Beantowners, who were victimized by Montreal six times, including three Cup showdowns. In all, Montreal defeated Boston six times in the final series during the streak. The tally is humbling: Montreal won 69 games, Boston, 22, while in the 91 games Montreal suffered only five home-ice defeats. One can imagine that the Bruins got very tired of hearing the Forum reverberate with the traditional victory song—"Les Canadiens Sont Là."

AGE OF YOUNGEST NHL PLAYER

16 years, 11 months: Bep Guidolin,
Boston Bruins, November 12, 1942

The onset of World War II opened the doors of the NHL to a lot of unlikely prospects, as established stars left to serve overseas. And in 1942–43, the Boston Bruins, who were in dire need of bodies to fill roster holes, embarked on a youth kick. Coach Art Ross put together the Sprout Line, composed of 19-year-old Bill Shill, 17-year-old Don Gallinger and Armand "Bep" Guidolin (who was only 16 years and 11 months old when he made his debut in a 3–1 loss to Toronto on November 12, 1942). Guidolin earned his distinctive nickname in childhood. He was the baby of the family, and his mother, who spoke Italian and very little English, pronounced baby as "beppy." The moniker stuck and was shortened to "Bep." Guidolin, who joined Boston directly from the junior ranks, scored his first NHL goal on November 24, 1942, against Chicago's Bert Gardiner, setting a record for the youngest NHL goal scorer. He connected again in the playoffs, seting a record for the youngest playoff scorer as the upstart Bruins advanced to the finals before being swept by Detroit. Guidolin played nine seasons with Boston, Detroit and Chicago, where he became an avid supporter of the creation of a players' union, a move that abruptly ended his NHL career in 1952.

MOST POINTS BY A FAMILY IN ONE SEASON

316: Brent, Brian, Darryl, Duane, Rich and Ron Sutter, 1984–85

Greater names may have graced hockey history, but no family is more famous for populating the NHL with its progeny than the Sutters of Viking, Alberta. Grace and Louis Sutter had seven boys in nine years, and six of them made it to the NHL. It's hard to believe that many siblings could break into the world's best hockey league and collectively play more than 5,000 games. How Brent, Brian, Darryl, Duane, Rich and Ron went from a remote farming community to the bright lights is legend, one that has as much to do with upbringing as it does with ability or opportunity. Each youngster took the same path, playing junior for Lethbridge and Red Deer while scraping out a reputation for hard work, dedication and dogged determination, qualities they learned as boys on the family farm. Their grit and spirit produced the classic "Sutter" game: a scrappy sort of skill that they honed by working relentlessly on their shortcomings. None had the talent to capture an individual record, but together they managed to score more goals in one season than any other family unit (138 in 1983–84 and 1984–85), amass a record 316 points (in 1984–85, Brent scored 102; Brian, 74; Ron, 45; Duane, 41; Darryl, 38; and Rich 16) and win six Stanley Cups between them from 1976 to 2001.

LONGEST REIGN AS CAPTAIN

19 seasons: Steve Yzerman, Detroit Red Wings, 1986–87 to 2005–06

When Steve Yzerman joined Detroit in 1983–84, the franchise was in sad shape, having missed the playoffs in 12 of the previous 13 years. The youngster had an instant impact, setting team records for goals by a rookie (39) and points (87), finishing second to Buffalo Sabres goalie Tom Barrasso in the Calder Trophy voting and making the NHL's All-Rookie team. He also skated in the All-Star game after only half a season in the league, making him the youngest player to don an All-Star sweater. Then, just prior to the 1986–87 season, stating that he "wanted a guy with the Red Wings crest tattooed on his chest," coach Jacques Demers named the 21-year-old captain. The next year, Yzerman sparked Detroit to its first division title in 23 years. He would wear the "C" until his retirement two decades later, leading by example and winning three Stanley Cups. Stevie Wonder played 1,514 regular-season games, scored 692 goals and 1,755 points (the sixth-highest tally in NHL history) and became famous for his clutch performances. "The bigger the game, the better he played," said long-time teammate Kris Draper. One of Detroit's most popular pro athletes, the soft-spoken player known simply as "the Captain" had his No. 19 raised to the rafters by the Red Wings on January 2, 2007.

ACKNOWLEDGEMENTS

Thanks to the following publishers and organizations for the use of quoted and statistical material:

· *The Game* by Ken Dryden. Published by Macmillan of Canada. 1983.
· *The Hockey News*, various excerpts. Reprinted by permission of *The Hockey News*, a division of Transcontinental, Inc.
· *The Official NHL Guide and Record Book.* Published by Total Sports Canada. 2006, 2007.
· *Total Hockey* (second edition) by Dan Diamond and Associates. Published by Total Sports Canada. 2000.
· *Total NHL* by Dan Diamond and Associates. Published by Total Sports. 2003.
· *Total Stanley Cup* by Dan Diamond and Associates. Published by Total Sports Canada. 1998, 2000.
· The *Associated Press; Canadian Press; Edmonton Journal; Globe and Mail; Montreal Gazette; Montreal Star; National Post; Ottawa Citizen; Toronto Sun; Washington Post;* and *Sports Illustrated, USA Today.*

Also, numerous other books and publications both guided and corroborated our research, including *A Breed Apart* by Douglas Hunter; *Century of Hockey* by Steve Dryden; *Gretzky: An Autobiography* by Wayne Gretzky with Rick Reilly; *Hockey: A People's History* by Michael McKinley; *The Hockey Scouting Report* (various years) by Frank Brown and

Sherry Ross; *In the Crease* by Dick Irvin; *The Last Hurrah* by Stephen Cole; *The Rules of Hockey* by James Duplacey; *The Trail of the Stanley Cup* by Charles L. Coleman; *Players: The Ultimate A-Z Guide* by Andrew Podnieks, and *What's the Score?* by Liam McGuire.

Finally, the authors gratefully acknowledge all the help throughout the years from Jason Kay and everyone at *The Hockey News*; Gary Meagher and Benny Ercolani of the NHL; Craig Campbell, Phil Pritchard and Steve Poirier at the Hockey Hall of Fame; Jon Trzcienski and Marie-Eve Sylvestre at the Club de hockey Canadien; Mike Leonetti of the Harold Barkley Archives; the staff at the McLellan-Redpath Library at McGill University; Rob Sanders and Susan Rana at Greystone Books; designers Peter Cocking and Jessica Sullivan; the many hockey writers and broadcast-journalists who have made the game better through their own work and contributions to various media and Internet organizations; statistical resources such as the Elias Sports Bureau, nhl.com, hockeydb.com, cbc.com, eurosport.com, hhf.com, shrpsports.com, espn.com, sportingnews.com and bodoglife.com; inputter Joy Woodsworth; and editor Anne Rose for her dedication, expertise and creativity.

PLEASE NOTE: Care has been taken to trace ownership of all copyright material contained in this book. The publishers welcome any information that will enable them to rectify any reference or credit in subsequent editions.

PICTURE CREDITS

CANADIAN PRESS

The Canadian Press (Tom Pidgeon)
page 27: Scotty Bowman
The Canadian Press (Jerry S. Mendoza)
page 51: Brian Boucher
The Canadian Press (Gregory Smith)
page 145: Roberto Luongo

CLUB DE HOCKEY CANADIEN

Denis Brodeur/Club de hockey
Canadien Inc. page 23: Henri Richard

CORBIS

Bettmann/CORBIS
page 92: Bill Cook; page 113 (left to
right): Lionel Hitchman, Myles Lane,
George Owen, Eddie Shore
Reuters/CORBIS
page 97: Martin Brodeur

DETROIT NEWS

David Guralnick/The Detroit News
page 152: Steve Yzerman

THE GAZETTE

The Gazette (Montreal)
page 15 (left to right): Dickie Moore,
Bernie Geoffrion, Toe Blake,
Maurice Richard

GETTY IMAGES

Bruce Bennett/Getty Images
page 4: Wayne Gretzky;
page 83: Tiger Williams
DK Photo/Getty Images
page 24: Mario Lemieux
J. Leary/Getty Images
page 31: Patrick Roy
Jim McIsaac/Getty Images
page 48: Sidney Crosby;
page 116: Brad Richards;
page 136: Alexander Ovechkin
Marc Serota/Getty Images
page 64: Evgeni Malkin vs.
Florida Panthers
Kellie Landis/Getty Images
page 110: Pavel Bure
Al Bello/Getty Images
page 140: Brian Leetch

HAROLD BARKLEY ARCHIVES

Harold Barkley Archives c/o Mike Leonetti
page 44: Bobby Hull vs. Toronto
Maple Leafs

HOCKEY HALL OF FAME

Graphic Artists/Hockey Hall of Fame
page 7: Gordie Howe vs.
Toronto Maple Leafs; page 133:

George Armstrong and Toronto
Maple Leafs
Frank Prazak/Hockey Hall of Fame
page 8: Glenn Hall; page 56: Tony
Esposito; page 120: Jean Béliveau vs.
Toronto Maple Leafs; page 148:
Bobby Orr vs. Henri Richard
Lewis Portnoy/Hockey Hall of Fame
page 12: Bobby Orr; page 18: Darryl
Sittler; page 35: Bobby Clarke,
Bill Barber; page 63: Bryan Trottier;
page 77: Phil Esposito; page 86: Garry
Unger vs. New York Islanders;
page 98: Paul Coffey; page 104: Ken
Dryden; page 107: Reggie Leach;
page 124: Mario Lessard
James Rice/Hockey Hall of Fame
page 32: Joe Malone
O-Pee-Chee/Hockey Hall of Fame
page 37: Teemu Selanne
Imperial Oil-Turofsky/Hockey Hall of Fame
page 40: George Hainsworth (left), Roy
Worters (right); page 52: The Produc-
tion Line (Gordie Howe, Sid Abel, Ted
Lindsay); page 67: Terry Sawchuk vs.
Toronto Maple Leafs
Paul Bereswill/Hockey Hall of Fame
page 68: Joe Sakic; page 72: Denis
Potvin and New York Islanders

Hockey Hall of Fame
page 80: Tiny Thompson
Doug MacLellan/Hockey Hall of Fame
page 59: Brett Hull
Dave Sandford/Hockey Hall of Fame
page 103: Dominik Hasek

SPORTS ACTION IMAGES
Sports Action Images
page 91: Gerry Cheevers

SPORTS ILLUSTRATED
David E. Klutho/Sports Illustrated
page 43: Wayne Gretzky vs.
Edmonton Oliers
Neil Liefer/Sports Illustrated
page 119: Stan Mikita
John G. Zimmerman/Sports Illustrated
page 128: Jacques Plante vs. New
York Rangers

INDEX

DON WEEKES is an award-winning television producer at CTV in Montreal. He has written numerous hockey trivia books, including co-authoring the Unofficial Guide series.

KERRY BANKS is an award-winning magazine writer and author. He has published 15 books on sports and resides in Vancouver.

Recipe for
good parenting

RYLAND
PETERS
& SMALL

LONDON NEW YORK

Cheryl Saban Ph.D.

Recipe for good parenting

words of wisdom *for* parents of all ages, *from* parents of all ages!

First published in the United States
in 2007 by Ryland Peters & Small, Inc
519 Broadway, 5th Floor
New York, NY 10012
www.rylandpeters.com

10 9 8 7 6 5 4 3 2 1

ISBN-10: 1-84597-510-3
ISBN-13: 978-1-84597-510-4

Printed and bound in China.

Senior designer Toni Kay
Commissioning editor Annabel Morgan
Picture research Emily Westlake
Production Clare Hennessy
Publishing director Alison Starling

Contents

Introduction

Parenthood is the one job on earth that seems to occur naturally, often without much effort or study, usually with a certain level of joy, and perhaps with a defining moment of exhilaration. And most of us feel entitled to achieve it. Yet this occupation, job, duty, honor, blessing, and/or miracle requires more strength, patience, love, selflessness, and energy than any other endeavor we may ever undertake. You will be rewarded with the highest of highs and the lowest of lows. And guess what? You wouldn't give it up, not if your life depended on it.

Being a good parent means being a multi-tasker. You're able to function while sleep-deprived. You're an executive during the day, but you change dirty diapers at night. You have all the answers one minute, then suddenly discover you still have something to learn … from a nine-month old! Parents are a special group of individuals. Once you gain membership, you are signed in for life. And although it's a wild rollercoaster ride, it's well worth the price of admission. So, there you have it. Take these words of wisdom with a smile, a pacifier, a handful of Cheerios, and a wet wipe … and welcome to the club!

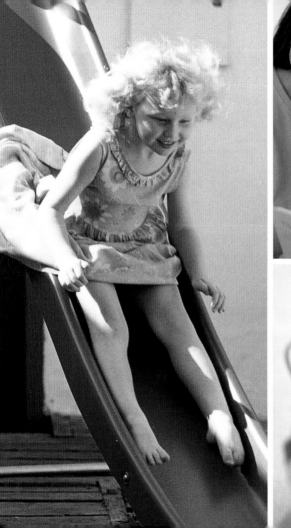

Recipe for good parenting

Visit your child's school • spend time with your child • monitor your child's television viewing • remember that laughter is a great healer • give your child the opportunity to explore • share a cuddle and a giggle every single day • be flexible! • respect your child • encourage sports • remember that music is good for the mind • read to your child • teach them the right values • find a common interest • delight in their discoveries • ask them to help • keep the promises you make • ask for their opinion, and care about it • notice them! • love them no matter what • accept them just as they are • expect them to do their best, but don't expect perfection • have patience with them • tell them you are proud of them • tuck them into bed at night • have family dinners • listen to their stories • appreciate their creativity • apologize when you are wrong • learn what your children have to teach you • remember to keep things in perspective • play with your child • don't let anger guide your actions • be understanding • encourage them to reach for their goals • love them • love them • love them • love them • love them • love them • love them • love...

9

Building confidence

Encourage your kids to reach for their *own dreams*, and give them the security of knowing that they'll be *loved* even if they sometimes fail.

Give your children
confidence.

13

Don't always
demand perfection.

$\mathcal{W}$hat is perfection, anyway? Remember that *every child* is unique, different, and special in his or her own way. Celebrate that specialness in *your child*, and just expect the best they can be!

Good parenting
requires *patience*
and a sense of
humor ... even
at 3 A.M. in
the morning.

Give unlimited
hugs and kisses.

Show your child
the world!

$\mathcal{L}$et your child try new
experiences and enjoy the world
around them. $\mathcal{S}$elf-esteem and
self-confidence is derived from
personal discoveries and
individual triumphs.

Be your child's *advocate*,
not his or her *adversary*.
From time to time, they need
to experiment, and they may—
(will)—test their boundaries.
Try to put yourself in their
shoes, and be understanding.

Remember what it was like to be a child.

Give positive
feedback.

$\mathcal{W}$e learn and grow and are willing to change because we *want to*—not because we are bullied into it. You can help promote your child's self-esteem and confidence. Point out the *good* things, rather than the bad. Give *praise* to your children rather than disapproval. (By the way, this works for adults too!)

Though our children *depend* on us completely when they are young, our challenge as parents is to imbue them with the skills and confidence they need to leave us one day, and become *independent*.

Parenthood does not
equal ownership.

Listen to your children!

Duh! This is a no-brainer. In a nutshell, *laugh* with them, read to them, eat with them, play with them, run in the grass with them, tickle them, *cuddle* them to sleep at night, give them your attention, and *love* them. Your children will thrive ... and you will too.

27

Happy families

Allow your children to be *who they are* and not only what you *hope* or *desire* them to be.

30

Let it be.

31

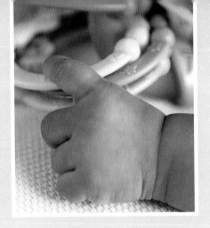

Give them time...

Carve out *at least* 30 minutes to be with your child each day—without the usual interruptions of cell phones and other avoidable distractions. *They* will always remember that you made this effort, and *you* will be blessed with the greatest of memories!

33

Children may fall, and they may bump their heads. We can't *protect* them from all of life's difficulties ... nor should we, for this could result in a learned sense of helplessness. However, we can be there with a Band-Aid and *a hug*.

Accept the fact
that there will be
growing pains.

35

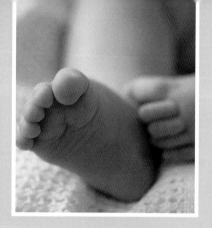

Be strong, wise,
and kind.

And also be fair. You may be bigger and stronger, but *you* can also make mistakes. So, buck up and apologize to your children when *you* are wrong.

$\mathcal{C}$hildren learn from example. Show *love* and compassion to your spouse or other half, as well as to yourself, and your children will *pick up* the habit!

38

Love your spouse.

Teach your children values.

Practice what you preach, and your kids will pick up on it. *Respect* others, take your responsibilities seriously, be compassionate, care about your community, and show *good faith*.

The kitchen is the heart of the home, and everyone likes to feel pampered once in a while. Comfort foods like French toast and choc chip cookies can turn a child's frown upside down!

French toast

2 eggs
1 cup (240 ml) low-fat milk
1 teaspoon vanilla extract
2 slices sourdough bread, or whole wheat bread

Mix the eggs, milk, and vanilla in a bowl. Soak the bread in the liquid, then sauté in a buttered saucepan until golden brown. Serve warm with butter and maple syrup, or scatter with sliced strawberries and a dusting of powdered sugar.

Chocolate chip cookies

2 sticks (225 g) butter
3/4 cup (140 g) brown sugar
3/4 cup (150 g) granulated sugar
2 teaspoons vanilla extract
2 eggs
1 cup (125 g) unbleached white flour
1 cup (125 g) whole wheat flour
1 teaspoon salt
1 teaspoon baking soda
2 cups (300 g) semi-sweet chocolate chips
If nuts can be tolerated, add 1/3 cup (40 g) of chopped pecans

In a bowl, mix the butter, sugar, vanilla, and eggs well. Beat in the flour, salt, and baking soda. Stir in the chocolate chips, and the nuts, if adding. Preheat your oven to 350 (180) Gas 4 and bake for 10 minutes. Yummy!

Learn to cook
something yummy!

Give unconditional love.

Try not to let anger guide your actions ... and remember that *unconditional love* goes hand in hand with *boundaries.*

It's not always the *quantity* of time, but the *quality*.
A goodnight story, and a hug, a kiss, and a snuggle can help
a little one feel secure and
settle in for *sweet dreams*.

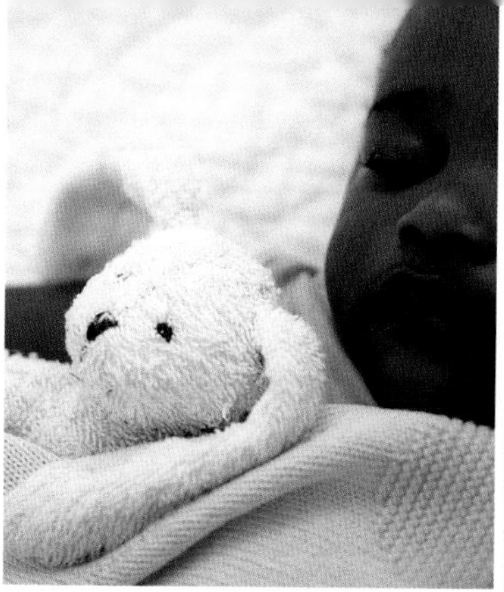

Tuck your children
in bed at night.

Teach them to give back.

The giver of a *gift* benefits as much, if not more, as the receiver of the gift. Teach your children to *give back* to society—to help others. Their lives will be enormously *enhanced* when they do.

Create an *emotional* connection cemented by respect, empathy, and a love that endures *always*, and in *all ways*.

Establish loving boundaries.

51

Staying sane

The mundane chores of *everyday life* can wear out new parents fast, putting everyone's fragile nerves on edge. Washing, cleaning, making beds, cooking meals, grocery shopping, kitchen clean-up … you get the picture. If you can't afford outside help, *share the burden*.

54

Take turns with household duties.

Learn tolerance and
understanding.

$\mathcal{L}$earn it quickly! This is particularly important when you find you need to *tolerate* a child's repetitious pounding on a toy drum, or to *understand* the incessant, unyielding whine of a tired toddler.

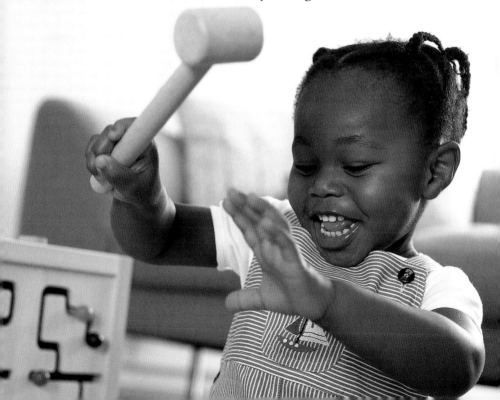

Believe it or not, your folks may have one or two *good ideas* to share with you. And if for some reason you can't call your parents, call another parent and/or your pediatrician. Bottom line, *it's okay* to ask for help!

When in doubt, call your parents for advice.

Keep things in perspective!

Try to look at the *bigger picture*.
The terrible twos will pass, your son
will eventually be potty-trained ...
and your daughter *won't* be sucking
on her pacifier on her wedding day.

61

Change is inevitable. Kids change, we change, ideas change, rules change. We can't control *everything* that happens. However, we *can* control how we *react* to what happens.

Be flexible.

63

Picture credits

Daniel Pangbourne: endpapers; pages 2; 7; 8; 15; 18 inset; 22 inset; 24–6; 30; 45; 50; 56–58.

Polly Wreford: pages 1; 3; 5; 10–12; 14; 17 inset; 20–21; 26 inset; 35; 36 inset; 41–44; 46 inset; 51; 55.

Debi Treloar: pages 4; 6; 8 left; 13; 17; 21 inset; 23; 28; 31; 39; 40 inset (*Catherine Chermayeff & Jonathan David's family home in New York, designed by Asfour Guzy Architects*); 48 inset; 49; 51 inset; 59–60; 61 (*Vincent & Frieda Plasschaert's house in Brugge, Belgium*) 62; 63.

Caroline Arber: page 39 inset; 46 (*Caroline Zoob*); 47 (*patchwork blanket by Olga Tyrwhitt*); 54 (*apron Caroline Zoob; rolling pin handles painted by Liz Crowther*); 63 inset.

Dan Duchars: pages 16; 19; 27; 52.

Winfried Heinze: pages 32 inset; 35 inset; 37.

Stockbyte (© Stockbyte): page 33.